Mysterious Mr. Darcy

A Pride & Prejudice Variation

Monica Fairview

Cover designed by Jane Dixon-Smith

Monica Fairview
Visit my website at www.darcyregencynovels.com

Printed in the United States of America

First Printing: March 2018
White Soup Press

ISBN-13 978-1-9804747-6-0

Other Darcy Books by Monica Fairview

Mr. Darcy's Pride & Joy
Mr. Darcy's Pledge
Mr. Darcy's Challenge
The Other Mr. Darcy
The Darcy Cousins
Steampunk Darcy

Other Regency Books by Monica Fairview

Dancing Through the Snow
A Merry Christmas Chase
An Improper Suitor

Prologue

October 1814

Bingley settled his feet on the medieval tapestry foot stool and stared glumly at his boots. "Confound it, Darcy! It's time you stopped brooding and joined society again. It's been six months since you returned to England, more than enough time to recover from your wound. Besides, I need you. I don't know anything about running an estate."

"You know very well it's out of the question."

Darcy tossed back his glass, rose, and walked to the window. The rain had stopped, and the remaining clouds were being ushered away by the wind. With the sun preparing to set, the outline of the iron age fort on top of the hill to his left stood rugged against the orange sky. The ivy covering the stone façade to his right was bathed in the golden light that he had come to associate with Cornwall. The old Cornish cross in the sunken gardens in front of him cast a long shadow across the grass. He liked the view, despite the circumstances, but he would never be able to call this home.

It was cold for this time of the year, too, with a bitter wind blowing down from the moors. The cold bled into Darcy's bones and leeched all the warmth out of them. It was impossible to keep the draught out in an old castle like this. The fire in the giant fireplace was doing very little to dispel the cold, and both the wound on his knee and the older one on his shoulder were aching. He hoped this was because he had only recently recovered and not a sign of things to come. He was far too young to be noticing aches and pains. It was this wretched seclusion. It made him dwell on every little thing.

It was good to have company, even if Bingley's visit was unsettling. Darcy had started to resign himself to being alone in this remote place, and it felt strange to see his old friend for the first time after Darcy's three-year absence on the Continent. Still, Bingley's presence had cheered him no end, and the brandy bottle they had consumed had helped him over the initial awkwardness. They had even laughed as they reminisced about some long-forgotten episodes at school. It had dispelled some of the grey mood that was haunting him, but only a little.

What Bingley was asking of him, however, was impossible.

"I would love to help you, Bingley, especially since I know how long you've been planning for this moment. I would really have liked to be by your side, but with the circumstances being what they are—."

"Damn the circumstances." It was Bingley's turn to tip back his glass. "You surely don't intend to exile yourself in your uncle's Cornish estate forever."

Darcy sighed. "No, not forever, but for as long as it takes."

There was a long silence – a silence unusual for Bingley. Curious, Darcy turned to look at his friend. He found him staring into his empty glass with an uncharacteristically solemn expression. What had happened to Bingley during his exile? He had never thought of Bingley as one of the people who would suffer because of his mistake, but he could see it had taken its toll on his friend's sunny disposition.

"The devil of it is, now that I have it, I don't really care about my new estate. I took it because Caroline insists that, if I'm to be viewed as a gentleman, I have to have one. She's got a bee in her bonnet about it. It's become almost an obsession, especially since she hasn't married yet. I know it's important to have an estate, but Mr. Hurst married Louisa, and I didn't have an estate at the time."

Darcy refrained from answering that Mr. Hurst was hardly what you would call a good match. True, he was a gentleman, and he resided in the fashionable area of town, but that was as much as could be said for him. At least he was too indolent to treat his wife badly. Still, he spent most of his time sleeping, which hardly made for good company, or any company at all. At times Darcy couldn't help feeling sorry for Louisa. Still, she seemed happy enough, or had seemed happy the last time he'd met her. There were still no children though. Perhaps Mr. Hurst was too lethargic to produce any heirs.

Tickled in spite of himself, Darcy couldn't help chuckling.

"I don't know why you think that's funny, Darcy."

"I don't think Hurst has enough energy to be bothered about anything. I'm surprised he made enough effort to be married. He must really care for Louisa."

Bingley's brow cleared, and he grinned. "Do you know, Darcy, I think you're right, though you'd never guess it by looking at him. I just hope Caroline finds someone who can love her for who she is, too."

Darcy could not imagine anyone falling in love with Caroline. She was too arrogant, for one, and was entirely too critical of everyone around her. There was a time, in his youth, when his friendship with Bingley had brought them together often, and Darcy had briefly considered an alliance. Caroline was pretty, and she had gone out of her way to engage his attention. He had been awkward and envied her the social graces she had learned at that expensive finishing school she had attended.

However, that had been some time ago. He now wondered what his younger self had seen in her, and from what Bingley had told him through letters and in person, she was becoming more interfering, and seemed to be managing Bingley's life more than she ought to. Bingley had always been disinclined to oppose her, even if she was his younger sister. His even-tempered character made him open to persuasion. Caroline, on the other hand, tended to be single-minded in pursuit of her goals, and at times Darcy wished Bingley would stand up to her more often.

In this particular case, however, Darcy agreed with her about the importance of the estate. Bingley's money came from trade – there was no escaping that. But for the next generation, having an estate was essential if they wanted to hold their position on the higher echelons of society.

"We all deserve to be loved, Bingley, but society defines who we are. It judges harshly." He was no longer certain if he was talking about Caroline or about himself.

Bingley made an impatient gesture. "That's neither here nor there. The fact is, I'm in a deuce of a spot. I have no experience at all of running a large estate. I wouldn't know where to begin."

"You're a quick learner. Hire a good steward and he will teach you everything you need to know."

"Or he could pretend to teach me, then fleece me of all my income. At least help me choose him. You will know what to look for."

Considering how casual Bingley was about most things, he seemed very insistent about this one. "I am beginning to think you came all the way here, not to see me, but to ask me to be your steward."

Bingley looked horrified. "Heaven forbid, Darcy! I would never think of you that way. You can't think—"

Darcy laughed at his confusion.

"Of course not. You would never hire me for a position. However, it is very likely that you pity me, and want to give me something useful to do, to distract me from my troubles."

The flush that stained Bingley's face showed that his words had hit the mark.

Bingley spluttered and began to stammer out some explanation.

"Don't insult me further by pretending otherwise, Bingley. I know you too well."

Bingley smiled broadly. "You are forcing my hand, Darcy. Very well, I will admit it. I'm not ashamed of it. But you're wrong about it being simply an excuse. I genuinely need help. Caroline can run a household – even if we have never had one quite so big – but she knows nothing about harvests and crops and modern agricultural methods. I bought some books and tried to read them, but I couldn't make head or tail of them, and every time I tried to read them, I fell asleep. So, you see, I do need an expert opinion. I have discovered that, unfortunately, you need to be raised a gentleman to be able to understand such matters."

Darcy thought about this, then nodded slowly. "Not all gentlemen are raised to manage estates. Only the heirs. But you have a point." He fell silent, considering various possibilities, then shook his head. "I'd ask my uncle to lend you his steward, but we are approaching the harvest season, and he will very soon be too busy."

"Exactly. So you see, it's a matter of some urgency for me. I have never had to deal with a harvest before."

The image of Pemberley, with the patchwork of gold and green on its rolling hills, rose up vividly in his mind. He had always loved this time of the year. A sharp pang of nostalgia stabbed at him, bringing with it the scent of freshly cut hay mixed in with scent of roses his mother had tended so carefully. He could taste the sweet-sour bite of apple on his tongue, picked from one of the trees in the orchard. He missed Pemberley with a profound sadness. He wondered how they were doing without him. What he would give to be there now!

It was the liquor speaking. He wasn't used to it any more. He'd lost the head for it. He didn't like to drink when he was alone, and he rarely had company these days. He put down the brandy. He'd had enough. He'd worked hard to put his regrets and memories behind him. He didn't want them resurfacing like this.

He needed to eat something. Drinking on an empty stomach was never a good idea.

"When on earth are they planning to serve dinner?" He walked over to the bell pull.

"It's not even five o'clock, Darcy." Bingley gave him a quizzical look. "Since when have you kept such early hours?"

"This is the country, Bingley. We do not keep London hours. Or have you forgotten?"

"Since I cannot visit you at Pemberley, I have few opportunities to spend time in the country."

There it was again. Pemberley. The ghost that seemed to be occupying the room with them.

"I wish you wouldn't compare the two. The wilds of Cornwall are nothing like Derbyshire."

"I disagree. Both are remote, and both have a wild beauty to them."

"I did not know you were fond of wild landscapes. Be careful, or you will sound like a romantic poet, Bingley."

Bingley grinned. "Not very likely, Darcy. But you know me. When I'm in the country, I like the country more than anything. Then when I'm in Town, I believe it to be superior to anything else. Still, you can't deny that Cornwell is beautiful."

"It has its appeal."

"But it's not Pemberley."

"No, it is not."

The grin had faded, and Bingley was regarding him with sympathy in his eyes.

"You must miss it."

The conversation was turning maudlin. It was time to put an end to it. "I hope you don't intend to keep badgering me with questions about the past, Bingley. I may not be inclined to answer them."

"No need to go into a high dudgeon, but you must know you can't stay here forever. Sooner or later, you're going to have to face the world and return from this self-imposed exile."

Sooner or later, you're going to have to face the world and return from this self-imposed exile."

They were back to where they had left off. At least, thought Darcy, this was a less wrought subject. "Just because you now have an estate, it doesn't mean I need to join you."

"But I had you in mind when I leased it. It is far enough from anywhere so that you can feel at ease, and with the nearby village being so small, there is little chance that anyone there will know anything about you."

It was tempting. Heavens knew he would do anything to end his isolation. But, no. It was too risky.

"I am sorry to refuse you, but I simply cannot."

"If you won't come out of your isolation to help me with my estate, then at least think of Pemberley."

"I thought I told you not to mention Pemberley."

"Someone has to mention it. Look, if you ask me, Darcy, I think you're making too much of the whole affair. Don't you think you have neglected Pemberley long enough?"

"Pemberley is not neglected. It is being taken care of, possibly better than I could care for it myself."

"How can you be certain, when you haven't even been to see it?"

"I trust my cousin Richard. He will take care of it even better than I could."

"So, what of the future? Do you intend to give up your right to Pemberley entirely? Who will the property go to? Like it or not, you are the last of the Darcys. If you don't marry, the Darcy name will die out. Are you willing to allow that to happen?"

"I have made my peace with the concept. It could very well have happened at the Battle of Toulouse." Darcy rubbed the scar on his knee.

Bingley shuddered. "Well, it didn't, so it's no use thinking that way anymore. You need to have an heir."

There was a silence in which Bingley's words twirled about in Darcy's head. When he had gone into exile, he hadn't cared, but was he still willing to let that happen now that he was back in England?

Bingley watched him, scenting victory. Darcy remained silent, ignoring his friend's scrutiny.

"So you see, Darcy, you have a reason to come to Netherfield."

Darcy shook his head and smiled. "So you think I'm to find a wife in – what was the name of the village? Merton?"

"Meryton, Darcy. And no, I don't suppose you will, but it would be a good way to re-enter society."

It was tempting – too tempting – but he could not allow himself to be lured. He had to stay steadfast.

"Enough, Bingley. If you will persist in this conversation when I have expressly forbidden you from doing so, I will have to ask you to leave."

Bingley flushed. "You wouldn't, Darcy."

"I would. I will not be questioned at every turn. My life is my own. I have made peace with my decision, and I have no intention of changing my mind. So I suggest we change the subject and make the best of your visit by occupying ourselves with something else. How about a game of pool? I have improved dramatically over the last three years. You will find it very difficult to defeat me."

Bingley was still predictable, Darcy was happy to see. He jumped to his feet at once.

"You may have improved, but so have I. I bet you twenty pounds that I will win."

"Are you certain you wish to part with your money?"

"Ah, but I will not."

Bingley laughed, and, to Darcy's relief, nothing more was said again that day about Bingley's new estate.

Chapter 1

No one could speak of anything else. Netherfield Park had been let at last to a young gentleman with a fortune of four to five thousand a year. The exact amount was uncertain, but it changed with every new telling. What *was* certain was that there had not been such a commotion in Meryton since, almost three years ago, Mr. Collins had proposed to his cousin Miss Elizabeth Bennet, who had turned him down. Without the slightest scruple, Mr. Collins had immediately rushed out to propose to Elizabeth Bennet's best friend, Charlotte Lucas, who had accepted his offer with equal haste.

Since that day, very little had happened to disturb the tranquility of the sleepy neighborhood. Two other young ladies had married, one of them Miss Elizabeth Bennet's sister Jane, the other one Miss Mary King, who was in possession of a small fortune. Neither wedding had captured the town's collective attention, since they had both been quiet affairs. Jane Bennet had married in London, and although Mrs. Bennet had tried everyone's patience by exclaiming over every detail of the ceremony, both before and after it had taken place, no one else in Meryton had had the pleasure of attending. Meanwhile, Mary King's wedding had been so small, it had been over before it had started, and Miss King had moved away at once.

Now, with the arrival of an eligible young gentleman, the town was humming with expectation. The Bennet family in particular was roused by the prospect. His arrival galvanized Mrs. Bennet's determination to see her girls well settled. Giddy with the certainty that one of her daughters would succeed in capturing Mr. Bingley's affections, Mrs. Bennet felt justified to break years of tradition by throwing open the door to the library and bursting into the room while her husband was reading.

"My dear Mr. Bennet," she said, with a sense of utmost urgency, "What are you doing here? You must call on Mr. Bingley at once!"

Mr. Bennet, who did not like to be interrupted in his sanctuary, looked up from his book and pointedly removed his spectacles.

"To what do I owe this unexpected intrusion, Mrs. Bennet? Why must I visit Mr. Bingley?"

"How can you be so tiresome, Mr. Bennet? You must know that I am thinking of his marrying one of my daughters."

"Is that his design in settling here?"

"Nonsense! Of course it is not, since he hasn't met them yet, but you must know it would be a remarkable thing if we could have one of our daughters married."

"One of them *is* already married, Mrs. Bennet."

Elizabeth Bennet, who was privy to this exchange, could not help smiling. Mr. Bennet delighted in vexing her mama, and mama never knew when she was being teased.

The mention of Jane, however, brought on the usual longing to see her. Dear Jane. If only she was here now! Elizabeth missed her sister terribly, especially on occasions like this, because she was the only person she could be entirely open with. She could have told her how bored she was of Lydia and Kitty droning on about the Assembly and how they hoped to capture Mr. Bingley. She was tired of hearing the new arrival spoken of everywhere.

Jane, with her good nature and tendency never to find fault in anyone, had always managed to talk Elizabeth out of her more scornful moods. At the moment, Elizabeth was inclined to think Mr. Bingley was a fictional character, nothing more than a figment of everyone's imagination. From what she had heard, he was impossibly handsome, elegant and amiable. In other words, he had been infused with every virtue under the sun. The real Mr. Bingley, she decided, was probably an unpleasant curmudgeon who had never received so much attention in his life.

Nevertheless, despite herself, Elizabeth was intrigued. She would be a fool to pretend otherwise. There must be *some* substance to the rumors. They couldn't be completely made up. She couldn't wait to find out for herself what this prodigy was really like.

If nothing else, watching the young ladies fawn all over him would provide enough amusement to last them several months.

∞ ∞ ∞

Mr. Bennet did call on Mr. Bingley, and he surprised Mrs. Bennet and his daughters by announcing suddenly one evening that, having met Mr. Bingley, he intended to give his blessing to whichever of his daughters Mr. Bingley chose to marry.

"I just hope he chooses Lizzy because, if they settle in Netherfield, she won't have to go away. I am reluctant to part with her. She is my only source of sensible conversation."

Mrs. Bennet was torn between triumph at knowing they could now secure an introduction to Mr. Bingley and vexation at Mr. Bennet's obvious bias towards Elizabeth.

"What nonsense you speak, Mr. Bennet! He might like any of our girls, except Mary, perhaps, because she is too plain. But if Lizzy wants to capture any man's attention, she has to smile more and speak less."

"Some would say I smile more than I ought," said Elizabeth, with a laugh.

"You don't smile. You laugh, which is entirely different."

Elizabeth braced herself, expecting Mrs. Bennet to continue for some time in this vein, but her mother had already lost interest in their conversation. The vexation had given way to delight.

"So we are now acquainted with Mr. Bingley. I can't wait to tell sister Philips. She was warning me just yesterday that if we did not make haste, Mrs. Long would know him before we did, and she would contrive to grab Mr. Bingley for her daughters. However, I was not worried. I always knew you would do the right thing, Mr. Bennet!"

Beside herself with joy, she began to inundate her husband with questions, but he escaped with his usual speed into the library and shut the door behind him.

They learned nothing more about Mr. Bingley, despite numerous attempts to draw Mr. Bennet out. Not even Elizabeth succeeded in wrangling a description of the gentleman from her papa. Mr. Bennet was enjoying being mysterious and was even more evasive than usual.

"But Papa, you can't claim not to know what he looks like. You are the only person in this family who has set eyes on him."

"Now, now, Lizzy, you can't have me spoiling the anticipation, can you? Besides, a gentleman in possession of a fortune is always fine looking, don't you think, especially if he is in search of a wife?"

"Papa, I hardly think a brief description will spoil my sense of anticipation. There will be plenty of things to look forward to in him, including finding out about his character."

"Well, if you must have it, Lizzy, I think he's a fine figure of a man. Will that satisfy you?"

"No, it will not, Papa, and you know it very well. I need a description from you."

"Need, Lizzy, or want?" Mr. Bennet looked at her over his round spectacles. "If you insist, I will tell you that he is of medium height, with hair that is light colored. His features are unremarkable other than that."

"What color are his eyes?"

"Come now, you would hardly expect me to have noticed his eyes. Men do not generally peer into other's gentlemen's eyes."

In the end, she had to be satisfied by her father's reassurance that Mr. Bingley was 'a handsome enough young fellow.' At least he wasn't wrinkled and old, which was hopeful. Beyond that, she couldn't judge whether her father was concealing something or whether Mr. Bingley was genuinely as cordial as they said.

Her curiosity aroused, she found herself looking forward to meeting the new arrival as eagerly as everyone else.

∞ ∞ ∞

As soon as it was apparent that Mr. Bingley would be attending the Meryton Assembly, Mrs. Bennet dug deep into the estate's almost empty coffers and ordered new ribbons, gloves, and trimmings for all the girls. It was too late to have new evening dresses made, and Mrs. Bennet bemoaned the fact hourly. However, Elizabeth was able to change the sleeves of her dress to fit the latest fashion, and, by stitching on some pearls and new lace, felt satisfied that the gown would be good enough for Mr. Bingley.

Only one matter cast a shadow on Mrs. Bennet's exhilaration. Mr. Bennet invited Mr. Bingley for dinner. After planning half a dozen menus in an effort to impress him – and not being able to decide which one – Mr. Bingley spared her the trouble of choosing. He sent round a note with his regrets, saying he needed to go up to Town that day.

"What business can it be that takes him to Town so soon after his arrival?"

Mrs. Bennet did not take kindly to the refusal and complained bitterly that he could have at least waited to go up to London until after the dinner invitation. However, she was soon ready to forgive him when Mrs. Philips had it on good authority that Mr. Bingley was bringing with him a London party of at least eight gentlemen.

As the night of the Assembly approached, the sense of expectancy grew stronger. Even Elizabeth -- who was convinced she was going to have her hopes dashed when she finally came face to face with Mr. Bingley – was infected by the fever. A party of eight was promising. It was infinitely better than the knowledge that all the single young ladies in Meryton would be competing for a single eligible gentleman.

Who knows, she thought, maybe I will finally encounter someone I could fall in love with. At four and twenty, Elizabeth was by no means as optimistic as she had been at twenty-one that she would encounter the man she was destined to marry. There was still time, of course, but leaving Longbourn to set up her own establishment was growing more and more appealing, particularly now that she no longer had either Jane's or her friend Charlotte's company. She did have a friend, Ruth Pratt, but Miss Pratt lived a little out of the way, so Elizabeth did not see her as often as she might have liked.

Mrs. Bennet's voice broke into her thoughts. "Lizzy! I asked you a question!"

Elizabeth looked up from working on her ball gown and found her mother and three sisters looking at her expectantly.

"Mama?"

"Your mind is always somewhere else, Lizzy, though I cannot imagine what you can be thinking of. You are too much like your father. That is what comes of reading so many books."

"I have the right to my own thoughts, mama," said Elizabeth, with a smile.

"Not when I am talking to you. I was saying that you must make a particular effort to attract Mr. Bingley's attention. You missed your chance to marry when you refused Mr. Collins. When I think of Charlotte Lucas being mistress of Longbourn—." She broke off to bring her handkerchief to her eyes. "Your father did you no favor by encouraging you to say no to him. Look at you now. Another year and you will have to wear a spinster's cap. I hope you don't plan to be particular about Mr. Bingley."

Elizabeth shook her head. "Mama, we do not even know if he will be interested in me."

"He's more likely to show an interest in me," said Lydia, stoutly. "I'm taller and more handsome. And besides, mama, Lizzy's already an old maid. Aunt Philips said so the other day."

"Take no notice of sister Philips. I am certain she only says this to vex me."

Elizabeth was at first taken aback by Lydia's remark, but she had too much of a lively, playful disposition to dwell on it. She delighted in anything ridiculous, and her mother's protestations at aunt Philips' remarks soon aroused her mirth.

"I do not think she could have said it to vex you, mama," she said, laughing, "since you were not there."

Mrs. Bennet, confronted with this logic, merely said darkly that, if Elizabeth had married Mr. Collins instead of letting Charlotte do so, she would not have been called an old maid at all.

Since Elizabeth had been hearing this refrain for some time now, it had no impact on her.

"If I had married Mr. Collins, I would have *looked* like an old maid. My hair would have turned white by now."

Lydia and Kitty giggled, while Mary looked as if she might produce a quotation on the subject of frivolity.

"Nonsense! How can you talk so, when he will be throwing us into the street the moment he inherits Longbourn?"

Elizabeth hid a smile. Her mother was so predictable. She could never miss an opportunity to bring up the issue of inheritance.

"Then you must endeavor to keep Papa happy, mama, to ensure he lives a long, healthy life," said Elizabeth. "Who knows, maybe, with your help, he will even outlive Mr. Collins. I do believe Papa has a more robust constitution than our cousin."

Mrs. Bennet, who had never been swayed by such an argument before, suddenly seemed struck by the idea. "Do you know, it is quite likely, Lizzy, because Charlotte has no idea of the right sort of food to give her husband. Besides, it is very possible the dinners at Lady Catherine's house are too rich, and will cause him to develop gout before he is thirty."

The idea pleased Mrs. Bennet so much that she hurried downstairs to advise Cook about what dishes to prepare for Mr. Bennet, leaving Elizabeth relieved to know she had escaped at least one lecture on her folly in refusing to marry Mr. Collins.

∞ ∞ ∞

Fitzwilliam Darcy stared out of the window, trying to make out the outline of Netherfield. So far, he had received a positive impression of Bingley's new estate. The land itself appeared to be prospering, and the few tenant's houses he had seen so far were in good repair. It was too early to tell, of course, especially as Darcy had not even seen Netherfield Place itself, but Bingley had apparently chosen well.

More importantly for him, it appeared that Bingley had been right about the location of Netherfield. The area was sparsely populated, and it was unlikely that Darcy would run into any of his acquaintances here.

Darcy could still scarcely believe that he had taken this step. During the long journey from Cornwall to Hertfordshire, Darcy had stopped the carriage twice. Each time, he had given the order to turn back. There were many reasons to stay in Cornwall, and very few reasons to leave. His mind argued that removing himself from Cornwall was unwise and could only lead to problems.

His heart, however, insisted otherwise. All he had to do was pick up the letter from his sister Georgiana he had placed next to him on the carriage seat – a constant companion on the road – and his determination to follow his original plan to join Bingley would strengthen. The letter would remind him why he was doing this, and he would order the coachman to resume the journey to Netherfield. The coachman, Darcy was convinced, must think him completely capricious. Even now, he wasn't sure he had made the right choice, but he was here now, and it was too late to change his mind. He only hoped this decision would satisfy his sister.

He and Georgiana had exchanged letters regularly over the last three years. His sister was a good correspondent, and her letters were always full of delightful details that painted a clear picture of life in Pemberley – Mrs. Reynolds hiring a new maid, Cook making the old dishes that he liked, the new rose bush that Georgiana had planted next to his mother's special breed. The letters made him homesick, but they were a lifeline. They enabled him to maintain an illusion that he was still connected to everyone there.

However, this letter was completely different. It had a different tone. It had shaken him to the very core. His belief that at least his sister was happy had been destroyed. That, too, apparently, was an illusion. How long had this been going on?

Dear Brother,

I hope all is well with you, and that you have recovered fully from your poor wounded knee. I wish Cousin Richard would allow me to visit you, or that he at least would travel to Cornwall to see you. I know the circumstances do not permit it, but it is so painful being here in the comfort of Pemberley, our own home, knowing you are living in an abandoned old castle in the middle of nowhere.

Dear William, there is something I have wanted to say for some time now, and I cannot keep it to myself any longer. I did not want to bring this up in my letters before, but now that your wound is much improved, and you are here in England, I cannot keep it to myself any longer.

The fact is, I am wretched. I am consumed by guilt. I wake up every morning, knowing that your life has been blighted because of me. You need not deny it. It is the simple truth. It is because of me that you have been forced to endure exile and isolation. I had hoped when you returned to England, things would be different, that you would be able to go out in society again. Now I realize that nothing has changed. I cannot bear it any more. I cannot continue to be the reason you cannot live your life in full. I must do something. I have not determined what it is, but I have resolved to find a solution.

Your devoted sister, Georgiana

When Darcy first read the letter, his blood had run cold. Georgiana's words had an ominous ring to them. What did she have in mind? What would her guilt drive her to?

He realized he had never really considered the impact of his exile on Georgiana herself. When he had left England, he had made certain his cousin, Colonel Richard Fitzwilliam, took responsibility for Georgiana as well as for Pemberley. It had seemed like the logical solution at the time, since Fitzwilliam was already Georgiana's guardian. Never in his wildest dreams would Darcy have thought that Georgiana would take the blame for everything that had happened.

As soon as he had read the letter, his immediate impulse had been to order his carriage and rush to Pemberley as fast as possible to stop Georgiana from doing something foolish. Fortunately, Bingley had been there to talk him out of it, and he now appreciated his friend's presence of mind. It would not help Georgiana at all for him to be arrested and imprisoned. He could not possibly return to Pemberley without everyone knowing of his presence.

Several hours and a restless night later, one thing became abundantly clear. He could not remain in Cornwall if Georgiana believed him to be miserable here. He could write to her and try to convince her, of course, but he did not think she would believe any of his protestations.

To make her feel better, he had only one course before him. If he could reassure her that he was living a normal life again, he would be able to relieve at least some of her anxiety.

He had no choice but to return to society again, it seemed. Bingley had been right after all.

Chapter 2

I t was the afternoon of the Meryton Assembly. Bingley's brother-in-law, Mr. Hurst, was sleeping in an armchair with his mouth open, punctuating their conversation with an occasional snore. Bingley's two sisters, Louisa Hurst and Caroline Bingley, were looking as if they would rather be in London. Darcy was wondering if he could excuse himself, claiming his was fatigued from the long journey. Meanwhile Bingley was talking enthusiastically about the Assembly.

"I think you will enjoy it, Darcy. It's a pity we haven't had the chance to tailor some new clothes for you, but I'm sure what you have is more than adequate for a country Assembly. They won't be as fastidious as they are in Town."

"I really have no desire to attend the village dance, Bingley." Darcy all but growled the words. If he had arrived just one day later, he would not have been compelled to be part of this ridiculous charade.

"I agree with you entirely, Mr. Darcy." Miss Bingley's voice was distinctly nasal. "I don't see why Charles is so insistent that we attend."

Bingley's cheerful disposition remained unchanged in the face of such opposition. He had been thrilled he had managed to convince Darcy to stay with him at Netherfield, and nothing Darcy or his sister Caroline could say could dampen his spirits.

"But, Caroline, there is no purpose in having an estate if you refuse to establish yourself in the neighborhood. It is part of my duty as a gentleman – and yours as a lady – to take your place among your equals. If you do not wish to do that, why did you insist on me leasing an estate? You can't have your cake and eat it, Caroline. Just say the word and I will give up the lease, return to London, and abandon the idea of a country living once and for all."

"But Mr. Darcy doesn't seem to think it's necessary, Charles, and he knows better than you do what gentlemen ought and ought not to do. Isn't that so, Mr. Darcy?"

Darcy cleared his throat. The fact that he didn't want to go to the dance had no bearing at all on Miss Bingley's situation.

"I am sorry to disappoint you, Miss Bingley, but your brother is perfectly right. As landowners, it is your duty to interact with other landowners in the surrounding areas. You will also have the responsibility of seeing to your tenants and helping the poor. It is what well-bred young ladies who live in the country are taught to do from childhood. Georgiana was expected to do the rounds when she came home from school, from a very young age."

The memory of young Georgiana coming home during the holidays wrenched at him, particularly now, after her letter. He had not seen her for so long. If only he could see her and explain to her that she was not to blame for anything that had happened. Her only fault was that she had been too young to know better. Unfortunately, it was not an option. The moment Miss Darcy of Pemberley arrived in Netherfield, his identity would be uncovered. It was beyond endurance. He closed his eyes and took a deep breath, cautioning himself to be patient.

Miss Bingley's groan of protest broke into his thoughts and he opened his eyes to find her pouting. "I have never understood this strange custom. Surely we can send the servants to enquire after the tenants and the sick. Why do we have to do it ourselves?"

This was the problem with not being born a gentlewoman. Other ladies knew what was expected, but Miss Bingley was always questioning the most obvious things. The two Bingley sisters had been to the best academy money could buy and had attended the best finishing schools. They behaved like proper young ladies, and had all the accomplishments they needed, yet there were always unspoken rules that would distinguish them from those who had been born to this life. They were traditions handed down from one generation to the other. Even the best Ladies' Academies did not adequately make up for that.

"It is an unwritten code of conduct, Miss Bingley – one of those things you are expected to know if you are bred to this position."

The situation was different in Bingley's case. Young boys were sent away to school at an early age and learned much about being a gentleman – apart from running an estate— at school. Bingley had attended Eton and that had equipped him well enough.

Miss Bingley pouted again. "Very well. You have convinced me that it is our duty to visit the poor. But that does not mean I have to attend the Assembly and expose myself to a crowd of unwashed nobodies, surely? We will be expected to dance with every uncouth gentleman in the vicinity."

"And to look as if we enjoyed it," added her sister Louisa.

Darcy would not have worded it quite this way, but he did agree with Caroline in principle. He disliked balls at the best of times, and to be forced to attend a room full of women thrusting their daughters at him was his idea of a nightmare. He was entirely in charity with Miss Bingley about this, at least.

"I see your point, Miss Bingley. I have never understood the appeal of these occasions. It would have been better for all of us if we had postponed our arrival."

Bingley rounded on him.

"I would have thought you would know better than to encourage my sister, Darcy. You are supposed to set an example of good breeding. Put yourself in my position. What would you do if you were master of Netherfield?"

Darcy thought of the endless Assemblies and dances he had been obliged to attend when he was at Pemberley.

He sighed. "Once again, Bingley, I would have to agree with you. I spoke out of turn. I am simply expressing my own disgust at the idea. Your duty requires—"

"Confound it, Darcy. This is not only about duty. It is the polite thing to do and you know it. It will actually be a pleasure to make the acquaintance of a room full of strangers who are intent on welcoming me to the district. I have already met some of the gentlemen, and they have all been very genteel and kind. I want to become part of the community."

That was what Darcy had always liked about Bingley – his willingness to throw himself wholeheartedly into any scheme he decided on. His perpetual good humor and eagerness to please those around him formed a frequent contrast to Darcy's own reticence to engage with strangers.

He might admire Bingley, but that did not mean Darcy was obliged to follow suite. He had been reluctant to come in the first place. He was not going to be dragged into this particular scheme.

"If you will forgive me, Bingley, but, while I commend your enthusiasm, I must refuse to accompany you. I have no intention of establishing myself in Meryton – far from it – and under the circumstances I do not wish to appear in public. I agree that your sisters have to accompany you, but you do not need me."

Miss Bingley shot him a resentful look. He ignored it. He had simply told the truth. She would have to embrace her new role or find herself snubbed by her neighbors. He hoped she understood the consequences.

"Oh, no, Darcy. You're not wriggling out of this one. What was the point of coming here from your exile in Cornwall if you plan to be a recluse?"

He should not have listened to Bingley's persuasions in the first place and agreed to come to Netherfield. Bingley had taken advantage of Darcy's distress at receiving his sister's letter and had finally convinced him coming to Netherfield was the wisest course of action. Darcy didn't doubt his decision to leave Cornwell, but he should have come up with a better location, somewhere where Bingley wouldn't badger him into being sociable.

"A recluse, Darcy. The whole reason you came here was to start mingling in society again."

Darcy vision of retiring early and having an evening to himself was looking less and less likely. "I don't suppose you will let me off if I promise to attend the next social occasion?"

"No, I will not. I've always been your social conscience, Darcy. You must allow me to be your guide about this."

Darcy had to acknowledge this was true. It was the reason they had become friends in the first place. At Eton, Darcy had given consequence to Bingley, who was considered an upstart because of his links with trade. In return, Bingley had guided Darcy through the bewildering complexities of social interaction. Bingley always knew what to do in awkward situations, while Darcy, being naturally reserved, found himself often giving offence without intending to. He did not like hypocrisy, and was sometimes too honest for his own good. Bingley had taught him to navigate his way without compromising his integrity and helped him through many uncomfortable encounters.

"Besides, how do you think it will look, if words spread that you were an eligible young man staying in Netherfield, but you didn't bother to attend the Assembly? I can assure you, it will give rise to a great deal of speculation and curiosity. People will want to know if you are hiding something. No, Darcy, if you really wish to avoid being the object of gossip, you have to make yourself as unnoticeable as possible. You don't want to stick out like a sore thumb."

That clinched it. The last thing he wanted was to have people asking questions about him.

"Very well. You win. I will attend the Meryton Assembly."

Miss Bingley tittered. "Thank heavens! Now Louisa and I will have someone to dance with."

Darcy wished Miss Bingley did not take for granted that he intended to dance, but he simply bowed and resigned himself to the inevitable.

"I will be happy to dance with both of you, providing there is a decent orchestra. I cannot abide dancing if the musicians are bad."

Miss Bingley gave him a coy look. "Oh, fie, Mr. Darcy! I now know you are not serious about dancing with us, sir! You know there is no chance at all that there will be good musicians at a provincial assembly. You must not make good music a condition for dancing, or you will not dance at all."

Darcy thought that it would be the best thing that could possibly happen, but he knew Miss Bingley was too bothersome to allow him that possibility. Besides, he was not such a killjoy as to refuse to dance completely at a country ball.

"Very well, Miss Bingley, I promise to dance with you and Mrs. Hurst, but no one else."

Miss Bingley looked triumphant and Mrs. Hurst looked satisfied. Meanwhile, Mr. Hurst, hearing the name, woke up briefly. "What—? Oh, it's you, Darcy," he said, then promptly went back to sleep.

With that matter settled, all that was left was for everyone to decide was how Mr. Darcy was to be introduced. After several minutes' discussion, they all agreed that Mr. Darcy's first name, Fitzwilliam, was too distinctive and could be found far too easily in Debrett's Peerage. Darcy would rather not have added even more subterfuge to his disguise by changing his name, but he was only too aware of the consequences of revealing his identity. In the end, he compromised by taking up one of his middle names. Of those three names, Frederick, George and John, John was deemed the best.

"John is a very respectable name, Mr. Darcy. It is not grand, of course, like 'Fitzwilliam,' which has a ring to it, but it is a good, solid English name and nothing to be ashamed of."

"More to the point," said Darcy, gravely, "it will not reveal who I am. George was my father's name, so it will inevitably lead to Pemberley, but John Darcy could be anyone. It is a common name."

"I only hope I do not forget and reveal your name by accident," said Miss Bingley.

"If you do, I will be out of here and back to Cornwall in no time. I cannot emphasize how crucial it is to keep this secret."

"Of course, Mr. John Darcy," said Miss Bingley, "but we will have to practice it all the time, to grow accustomed to it."

"We had better wake up Mr. Hurst and let him know what we have decided."

It took some time to rouse Mr. Hurst well enough to make sure he understood the importance of sticking to Darcy's new identity.

"Good," said Bingley, smiling in delight. "We have resolved all our problems. I only hope there will be some pretty young ladies I can dance with."

∞ ∞ ∞

Darcy was by no means as delighted as Bingley was, but it occurred to him that it might work to his advantage. No doubt Georgiana – as a young lady who undoubtedly enjoyed the idea of attending a dance – would be happy to know that he was taking part in some of the more trivial aspects of society.

With the excuse of wanting to give instructions to the valet he and Bingley shared about his clothes for the evening, Darcy withdrew to his chamber. Shutting the door behind him, he sat down at the escritoire in his room and wrote to his sister.

Dear Georgiana,

I have now arrived at Netherfield from Cornwall. Netherfield is a large estate east of the small town of Meryton. Bingley is very pleased with it. I have been helping him go through the books, which are in a bit of a muddle. He has a good head for figures, but he has no experience in estate business, so we have spent some time cloistered with his man of business in order to make some sense of what he can expect from the property.

Bingley's new residence is very fine, Georgiana. You would like it. It is not as big as Pemberley, but it is very well situated, and the rooms are very well furnished. The furnishings are much more modern, of course, than those at Pemberley. There are no heavy shells or fish-scale carvings anywhere in sight, you may be relieved to know, and as a result the rooms are far more bright and airy. If I wasn't so attached to those old relics, I would have them removed and replaced with lighter pieces. However, I must admit that the parlor, which was done in Hope's Egyptian style, is not at all to my taste. Caroline Bingley had those furnishings brought from London, and I have yet to come to terms with winged sphinxes, lions and Egyptian gods occupying the same room as I do.

I am growing accustomed to being here, away from my ancient castle, as you call it. It is so strange to be among friends again. I am happy to break my isolation, but I fear I have become a curmudgeon and I'm no longer fit for company. I am not as used to the demands of constantly keeping up small talk and looking for entertainment. I admit I find it makes my head hurt. I will get accustomed to it again, no doubt, but at times I yearn to have the house to myself.

Nevertheless, you will be pleased to hear, I will be going to the local Assembly at Meryton, and I intend to dance at least with Miss Bingley and her sister. I warn you, however, I will not dance with anyone else.

The wound on my knee no longer pains me at all – not even the long journey affected it – though I still feel some stiffness in my shoulder, which I am resigned to. I have grown accustomed to it after three years.

I am very glad to be back in lush, quiet hills of this part of England, with its stately oaks and cultivated fields. Cornwall has its own brand of beauty, but it is more harsh and unforgiving, though in many ways, I have come to like the tors and vales of the wild country.

The autumn colors are growing beautiful. The vibrant hues here remind me of the harvest season at Pemberley. I look towards the north sometimes and imagine myself taking the carriage up the Great North Road to Pemberley. I long to see it, my dear sister, as I long to see you.

I am eagerly awaiting your news. You are my link to Pemberley and your stories of the servants' antics and the details of your life there make me feel that I am still there.

Affectionately yours,
William

Darcy read over the letter and sealed it. Aware of servants' inclination to gossip, he did not send the letter to Georgiana directly.

Instead, he addressed it to plain Mr. Richard Fitzwilliam at the inn in Lambton, Derbyshire. Satisfied that if Bingley franked it no one could trace it to him, he rang for the footman and had the letter sent express. He disliked this subterfuge, but there was no avoiding it.

Hopefully, the letter should convince Georgiana that all was well, and there would be no more desperate letters from her.

Chapter 3

M r. Bennet refused to attend the Assembly with the rest of his family. He was satisfied that he had gone to enough trouble already by calling on Mr. Bingley and inviting him to dinner. He made it abundantly clear that he was now looking forward to a peaceful evening alone.

Elizabeth was sorry her father was not coming with them. He was the only one who wasn't caught up in the bustle of preparations, and she could usually count on him to make witty comments about the newcomers, but she could not persuade him to join them.

"I have no interest in watching all the young ladies making fools of themselves over a single young gentleman."

"It's not just one gentleman, Papa!" Lydia rolled her eyes. "There are eight of them. Just imagine. And all of them from London! La! I shan't know who to dance with first."

Mr. Bennet raised his eyebrow. "I rest my case."

Elizabeth laughed. "Are you entirely sure you want to forfeit the opportunity to make sport of it all? Think of what you'll be missing."

"I am not in the least worried I'll be missing something. In fact, I'm absolutely certain that I'll be obliged to hear every single insignificant detail once you've returned home."

At the last moment, just as they were about to set out for the Assembly, Mrs. Bennet tried one last time to convince Mr. Bennet to come.

"But Mr. Bennet, how can you be so inconsiderate? How are we going to meet Mr. Bingley if you won't introduce us to him?"

"If he is interested in any of our girls, he will seek an introduction from Sir William Lucas. He is the Master of Ceremonies, not I. It is his job to do the introductions."

"*Sir William*," said Mrs. Bennet bitterly, "will undoubtedly be too busy parading his own daughter Maria in front of Mr. Bingley to spare us a thought."

"Well then, Mr. Bingley will marry Maria, and that will be that."

"Oh! I see you are determined to ruin our girls' chance of marrying."

"I am not determined to do anything. I am merely hoping for some time to myself. Is that too much to ask?"

Seeing that her mother was growing more and more agitated, Elizabeth broke in.

"If we don't hurry, we will be too late to witness Mr. Bingley's arrival."

Mrs. Bennet realized she had wasted precious time trying to convince Mr. Bennet.

"Why are you dawdling, Kitty? We have to leave at once!"

Kitty blinked. "I am not dawdling, mama."

"Then make haste!"

It was only a mile from Longbourn to the Assembly Hall, but it took them an age to reach there. The line of carriages that had already arrived was long, and the Bennets were obliged to wait for their turn. Mrs. Bennet began to complain and wish they had left earlier, while Lydia and Kitty stuck their heads out of the window to peer at the occupants of the other carriages. Nothing that Mrs. Bennet said could stop them. It was only when Elizabeth told them their curls were becoming windblown that they brought their heads back in. By and by, the carriage crept forward to the entrance. It finally came to a stop and a footman came to open the door.

Mrs. Bennet poked Elizabeth in the back.

"Hurry, Lizzy. I don't want Mrs. Long's daughters to meet Mr. Bingley before we do."

Elizabeth was given a push as she descended, and her sisters tumbled out after her, presumably also subjected to Mrs. Bennet's poking fingers. Unlike Elizabeth, who preferred a more dignified exit, Kitty and Lydia giggled excitedly and took their mother's prompt as license to behave as giddily as they pleased.

"Come on, girls," said Mrs. Bennet, herding her daughters like a mother goose with her goslings. "Let's find Mr. Bingley."

∞ ∞ ∞

As Elizabeth entered the Assembly Rooms, she bit back a smile. She had never seen such a crush of people. The room was filled to the rafters. The mamas were out in full force, fussing and giving frantic last-minute instructions. The prospect of having several eligible and wealthy young gentlemen in attendance had driven them into a frenzy. Fashion plates had been studied, ribbons and lace had been purchased from as far away as the market town of Hitchin, and many a curl had been burnt with the curling irons in a desperate attempt to hold their shape.

Mrs. Bennet's rush to arrive, however, proved to be pointless, because the Mr. Bingley and his friends had not yet arrived.

"How very vexing of Mr. Bingley not to have arrived by now," said Mrs. Bennet, to her sister. "The orchestra is getting ready to start."

"It shows a definite lack of consideration, sister." Mrs. Philips fanned herself rapidly and stared fixedly at the doorway. "He must know that we are all counting on his presence."

Elizabeth left her mother and her aunt to their complaining and joined a group of young ladies, but the conversation was the same everywhere. No one could talk of anything else. Everything was on hold. The evening could not begin properly until Mr. Bingley had made an appearance. Sir William delayed the dancing as long as he could, but as the crowd grew restless, he was forced to order the orchestra to begin.

Elizabeth danced the opening set with Mr. Robert Eckles, a young man with round blue eyes and a red face. She had known him since childhood, and knew they had nothing in common. They exchanged pleasantries from time to time, but otherwise did not make much of an effort to converse. Mr. Eckles was a good dancer, fortunately, and Elizabeth was able to enjoy dancing.

As the dance concluded, Elizabeth looked around for another partner. There were very few young gentlemen she could dance with, but they were all otherwise engaged. However, there were some things she wouldn't do. When a white-haired widower who was going deaf, Mr. Rice, asked her to dance with him as he always did, she declined, as she always did, but with the usual sense of frustration. Turning him down meant, of course, that she could not dance with anyone else for that set. She had always found that rule of etiquette ridiculous. Why did a young lady have to deprive herself of dancing for half an hour just because she did not like that particular partner?

Sighing, she went to fetch a glass of ratafia and joined her friend Maria Lucas, who was also sitting out the dance.

"It appears the London party has forsaken us," she said. "I think they've returned to London and forgotten all about us."

Maria shook her head. "I have it on good authority that they are coming. I'm sure there's a perfectly reasonable explanation for their delay."

"You're always trying to find a reasonable explanation for everything, Maria, just like your sister." Elizabeth smiled affectionately at her friend. "But people like this London group may have decided not to grace us with their presence for some arbitrary reason. We may never know the reason."

"They *will* come." Maria spoke with conviction. "They are new to the area and they need to get to know their neighbors. They'll have no one to call on if they don't make the effort to acquire new friends."

"Perhaps they don't care to acquire friends in Meryton." Elizabeth was, in fact, certain that they were not coming at all.

At that moment a sudden hush fell over the Assembly Rooms. The music stopped, and every gaze turned towards the entrance. Five young persons, three gentlemen and two ladies, walked through the door and into the large hall.

The sense of disappointment was palpable as it became clear that there were fewer gentlemen than anticipated, but the ladies' spirits rallied quickly. Mothers and daughters simpered as the new arrivals walked by. The mothers noted the fashionable clothes of the ladies, memorizing the patterns to make sure their seamstresses would be able to produce something similar. The younger women observed the gentlemen from the corners of their eyes, trying to decide which of the three they preferred.

"Welcome, welcome!" Sir William Lucas rubbed his hands together and bowed, his loud voice carrying easily in the silence. "I shall be performing the introductions tonight. We have many pretty young ladies here who are eager to dance -- and some charming young gentlemen, too, of course."

One of the gentlemen stepped forward with an eager look, and Elizabeth gave him her full attention. This must be Mr. Bingley, she decided, judging from the vague descriptions she had received of him. He was a tall man with light brown hair brushed forward in the new fashion, and large blue eyes. He seemed genuinely happy to be there. Elizabeth had the feeling he was someone who made friends easily and was eager to please.

Could she marry such a person? It was certainly too early to form more than a first impression, but she didn't find anything to dislike. So far, there was no thunderbolt, no sudden sense of her world shifting in any way, but she would have to wait until they were better acquainted. It was pointless to consider the matter in any case. Mr. Bingley did not even know she existed. It remained to be seen whether he would notice her at all.

∞ ∞ ∞

He had done some foolish things in his life, thought Darcy, as he stepped into the Assembly Rooms at Meryton, but this had to be one of the worst. Bingley had assured him that there were not more than twenty-five families around Netherfield. His friend had even gone to the trouble of finding out everyone's names and written them down. Darcy had gone through the list carefully and had made certain there was no one he knew.

However, as he entered into the packed hall, he realized the room held far more than twenty-five families. There could easily be someone here that would recognize him. In fact, it was almost certain to be the case, with such a large crowd. Bingley had said it would be a small provincial dance. Who were all these people?

His muscles tightened, his pulse began to race, and his throat turned dry. The music and the dancing had stopped, and everyone was staring in their direction. It was like entering the field of battle before an engagement, knowing that this time, he could be chosen by the hand of death. Any moment now, he thought, disaster would strike. Someone would mention his real name or ask him about Pemberley and then everything would come crashing down.

Somehow, without even noticing what he was doing, he managed to follow behind Bingley, who was being guided forward by a hearty gentleman with a round paunch. He heard someone introducing him as Mr. John Darcy, of Cornwall, and he bowed like an automaton every time the name was mentioned. Meanwhile, his vision scoured the room, looking for danger.

"Tedious occasion, eh, Darcy?" said Hurst. "I hope they have a decent cardroom at least."

The comment was so mundane, so commonplace, that Darcy felt an absurd impulse to laugh. His nerves were at snapping point. Any moment now, the game would be up. The torment seemed to stretch on and on.

Suddenly, he spotted a familiar face at the back of the room. He froze. The man wasn't looking at him, but Darcy knew that profile. He tried to remember the man's name. Was it Ridgeway, or Ridgewell? What should he do? Should he stand his ground, or should he flee before it was too late?

He would stand his ground. What was the point of running away? Even if he tried to leave, the man could still see him and recognize him. It would better for Darcy to stay. Perhaps he could bluff his way through the encounter.

"Come on, Darcy. Keep up!"

Bingley's cheerful voice was an annoyance. Darcy kept his eyes fixed on Ridgeway, ignoring his friend's taunt. He willed the man to turn so the torment could end. He wanted to be done with it.

Then Ridgeway finally turned and looked directly at him, his brow raised in a question, only it wasn't Ridgeway. This man was a complete stranger.

The tension that was like a spike digging between Darcy's shoulder blades eased as he allowed himself to breathe again, but the near-encounter left him shaky. It wasn't over yet. It could still happen.

Slowly, as they continued down the room and no one called out his name, Darcy began to hope. They were almost at the end of the hallway by now. The music had started up again, and people were turning away. Slowly, the sea of gazes began to separate into individual faces. Darcy didn't recognize anyone. For the first time, he paid attention to the Master of Ceremonies, who was completely oblivious to Darcy's apprehension. Sir William was chattering happily to anyone who would listen, about the time he had been at Carlton House and about how his services to King George had earned him the honor of a knighthood.

Darcy's apprehension began to diminish, then dissipated all together. He was safe here. Apart from the Master of Ceremonies, as far as Darcy could tell, all the guests were provincials who didn't run in the first social circles.

His pulse returned to normal. He had been spared. He was safe now, but he rebuked himself for taking such a foolish risk. Not for the first time, he wished he hadn't come. He only hoped Georgiana appreciated his sacrifice.

Chapter 4

Fortunately, Sir William was waylaid on the way and distracted from his purpose, and soon Lydia and Kitty drifted off, their attention drawn elsewhere. Elizabeth sighed with relief. She was only too aware of how poorly her sisters' behavior reflected on her family, and she would rather not confirm Mr. Darcy's apparently poor opinion of everyone present.

Sometime later, Sir William appeared at her side again, but it was not Mr. Darcy he brought. It was Mr. Bingley.

"Mr. Bingley here has sought an introduction, Lizzy. He would like to ask for this dance. Mr. Bingley, I present to you Miss Elizabeth Bennet."

Light blue eyes smiled into hers. "Miss Bennet. Delighted to make your acquaintance."

"You already know my daughter Maria, of course."

"I should hope so! We danced together." Mr. Bingley bowed and turned to Elizabeth. "Miss Bennet, may I have the pleasure of this dance?"

"By all means, Mr. Bingley."

"I hope you do not mind my taking your friend from you," he said to Maria. "I promise to return her."

Maria smiled, and said she looked forward to it.

Elizabeth was aware of Mr. Darcy watching as she made her way with Mr. Bingley to the dance floor. She smiled brightly at Mr. Bingley and did her best to ignore his friend. Soon, she forgot all about him as she discovered that Mr. Bingley was not only an excellent dancer but was charming as well.

"Have you lived near Meryton all your life, Miss Bennet?"

"We live a mile away, in Longbourn. It is a very convenient distance. We walk to Meryton three or four times a week, weather permitting."

"Very commendable. I rarely walk. I go everywhere on horseback, but I daresay walking is even better for one's health, especially in the countryside."

"I love to walk, whenever I can. However, if you are at all fussy about your boots, I would not recommend it."

"Oh, I am not fussy about anything. Besides, a little bit of mud never hurt anybody."

He smiled at her warmly. There was something very appealing about Mr. Bingley. As the dance went on, she found him very easy to talk to, and was soon telling him how much she missed her sister Jane.

"Why don't you go to London more often to visit her?"

"My father does not like me to go away. He and I have a great deal in common, you see, and he misses me if I leave."

"He could go to London as well, surely?"

"That's the problem. He dislikes London and never wants to go there, even to visit my sister."

"What a pity! But if you should wish to go any time, you are welcome to borrow my carriage. It is well-sprung and will get you to London in no time."

"I appreciate the offer, Mr. Bingley, but I don't have plans to go to Town at the moment."

Their conversation continued in much the same manner throughout the dance. Mr. Bingley was invariably solicitous, and Elizabeth felt that he was willing to go of his way to help her. It was a novel sensation to talk to a gentleman who was so obliging.

Yes, thought Elizabeth, as the dance reached its conclusion, I could come to like Mr. Bingley very much indeed.

∞ ∞ ∞

Half an hour later, as she and Maria stood together observing the dancers, Elizabeth was still at a loss to find fault with Mr. Bingley. She had watched him interact with several people and concluded that it would take someone very critical to find fault with him. The only fault she could find was not with Mr. Bingley, but with herself. Much as she liked him, she could not quite imagine herself marrying him.

The trouble was, she wanted more out of marriage than simply convenience. Something inside her yearned for love. She was aware, of course, that she was expecting too much. Mrs. Bennet was always complaining that Mr. Bennet had spoiled Elizabeth for her role in life by encouraging her to read too much. It was very probably true. Elizabeth's father was very well read, but he was not a practical man. He was not fully involved in the everyday running of the estate, which was possibly why the estate produced so little income. Meanwhile, the Bennet family members were paying the price for his neglect. They were always having to perform little economies so they could continue to live within their means. They were not impoverished, exactly, but they could not order fashionable clothes without having to give up something else.

Jane had married reasonably, but not well enough to help her sisters or mother with anything more than a trivial amount of pin money. Three years ago, when Mr. Collins proposed to her, Elizabeth had been contemptuous of anyone who married for practical reasons. Now she was older and wiser. She had seen how her friend Charlotte managed her husband. Charlotte had even worked out the best way to interact with Lady Catherine, Mr. Collins' condescending and interfering benefactor. In short, although Elizabeth had predicted a disaster for her friend when Charlotte had first married, she had been proven completely wrong. Charlotte was perfectly content. She had her own household. She had a little girl and was increasing again, and she wasn't dependent on anyone for a roof over her head.

Still, every part of Elizabeth revolted at the idea of trying to capture a man for his property. She wanted love. But would love ever come her way? At three and twenty, it seemed to be less and less likely, and the prospect of having to endure her mother for the rest of her life seemed much more real.

Not that Elizabeth would marry someone like Mr. Collins even now. She shuddered at the very thought of it. However, if an opportunity arose for her to escape Longbourn and the constant lamentations of her mother at being saddled with four unmarriageable daughters with no dowry, Elizabeth would certainly consider it seriously. Mr. Bingley was a godsend, that is, if he was genuinely interested in her.

She chuckled to herself. The poor man had done nothing more than to dance with her, and already she was considering whether or not to accept his proposal. It was absurd.

"Why are you laughing, Lizzy?" Maria was looking at her quizzingly.

"I was thinking how true it is that a lady's imagination is very rapid; it jumps from admiration to love, from love to matrimony in a moment."

Maria gaze moved from Elizabeth to Bingley. "He does seem to be taken with you."

Elizabeth shook her head. "It was just a stupid fancy on my part, no more. It will take a great deal more to fix his interest, I assure you."

"Then, as my sister would say, you have work to do." Maria sighed. "Imagine what it would be like to marry someone with a property such as Netherfield. Imagine being the mistress of such a grand estate. You would be very lucky indeed if you managed to capture him, Lizzy."

"If I fall in love with him, I will not hesitate, but I will not deliberately set out to capture him in cold blood, Maria, whatever Charlotte's view of the matter may be. Having said that, if he did become sincerely attached to me, I would not discourage it, even if I was not in love with him."

It was Maria's turn to shake her head. "If you aren't careful, someone will snatch him from right under your eyes, and all for the lack of trying."

"I'm not desperate, Maria. Your sister did not marry until she was twenty-seven, so I still have some time to acquire a husband."

"I wash my hands off you, Lizzy. Don't say I haven't warned you. If you won't listen to me, I will not be held accountable."

"Why don't you set your sights on him yourself, then?"

Maria gave a wry smile. "I would, only I'm not as pretty as you are, and so far, he only has eyes for you."

∞ ∞ ∞

It appeared Maria was right, because not too long later, Mr. Bingley solicited Elizabeth's hand for a second dance. Since she was the first young lady to be asked twice, Elizabeth took to the dancing floor with many envious looks turned in her direction. There was little occasion for conversation this time, since the dance was a jig, but Elizabeth enjoyed herself, and laughed a great deal with Mr. Bingley. Once again, he proved himself a skilled dancer, and Elizabeth was sorry when the music stopped, and Mr. Bingley returned her to her friends.

There were very few eligible young men to dance with, and after the excitement of dancing with Mr. Bingley, Elizabeth wished she could have danced more. However, as there were not enough gentlemen to go round, she was left without a partner for the next dance. Still, it was a good opportunity to amuse herself by watching other people.

"Come, Maria," she said to her friend. "Let us make ourselves comfortable over there, where at least we sit down as we sip our ratafia."

At that moment, someone approached to invite Miss Lucas to dance, and Elizabeth was left to her own devices.

It was only as she sat down that she realized that Mr. Darcy was standing not too far away. The chairs were positioned so that he was turned away from her, and she could not see his face. It was a pity, because she would have liked to see him close up. From a distance, in the candlelight, his face was cast in shadow, giving him a mysterious appearance. But she could not observe him without turning her head and making it obvious.

If only Mr. Darcy had been more obliging, thought Elizabeth, with a flicker of frustration, then she might have been dancing instead of sitting there awkwardly, tapping her foot to the music.

∞ ∞ ∞

Darcy was feeling even more out of place than he had expected. At first, a few of the more determined mamas had approached him, their daughters in tow, but he had deterred them, as he always did. He had all the more reason now to discourage them. The less people noticed him, the better. He would stay at the Assembly for only as long as necessary to establish his presence and to deflect any speculation. Then he would return to Netherfield and hopefully not be obliged to see any of these people ever again.

However, as he stood watching, it occurred to him that, once the initial curiosity had passed, no one was noticing him. All eyes were on Bingley. All the usual fawning, flattery and obsequiousness was addressed to his friend. At first it amused him, then it piqued him, and as the evening continued, it vexed him. It should not have vexed him. After all, that was precisely why he had come here, of all places. He wanted to be inconspicuous. It was just that he was so accustomed to being sought after that it was oddly demeaning to realize that, when he was not Mr. Darcy of Pemberley, he was so little regarded. It was sobering to see how much of the attention he had always received was due to his fortune and how little to his own character. The irony was that he had wanted to be invisible when he came here, but now that his wish had been granted, he felt dissatisfied.

A part of him rejoiced in suddenly being a nobody. For the first time in his life, he was plain Mr. Darcy, ordinary Mr. Darcy, with nothing to recommend him. On the Continent, as a Cornet in the Cavalry, he had been a lowly officer, but he had still had a position of some responsibility, often taking over responsibilities that belonged to the lieutenant or even captain. The men depended on him. In Cornwall, too, he had been in charge of his uncle's estate, however small and remote it was. Here, however, no one depended upon him for anything. He could simply be himself.

The sensation was both terrifying and liberating. He was on unfamiliar ground. His identity in England had always been closely tied to being the master of Pemberley. Without it, he felt stripped of his armor, exposed and vulnerable. Yet there was also a sense of freedom in not being defined by the property he owned. Here, he was first and foremost a man.

As his emotions fluctuated between joy and apprehension, he did not notice that Bingley had come to stand next to him. Considering that he was supposed to be alert for the possibility of being recognized, this was not a very desirable outcome.

"Come Darcy. I hate to see you standing around by yourself. You had better dance."

"I will not. You know how much I detest it, unless I am particularly acquainted with my partner. At such an assembly as this it would be insupportable. Your sisters are engaged, and there is not another woman in the room whom it would not be a punishment to me to stand up with."

"I would not be so fastidious as you are," cried Bingley, "for a kingdom! Upon my honor, I never met with so many pleasant girls in my life as I have this evening; and there are several of them who are uncommonly pretty. Miss Elizabeth Bennet for example."

"Who do you mean?" Bingley indicated a young lady seated on her own not very far from him. Darcy turned around, and looked for a moment at her, until, catching her eye, he withdrew his gaze and coldly said, "She is tolerable; but not handsome enough to tempt me."

At this moment, a friend of Miss Bennet came up to her with a smile, beckoning. Miss Bennet rose, and the two moved away to another part of the hall. Darcy noticed that she moved with an appealing mixture of grace and energy.

"Not handsome enough? How could you say that? Really, Darcy! I will never understand you."

Bingley was at it again. He should know by now that Darcy didn't like strangers. Besides, he had never grasped the appeal of skipping around the room with a lady he didn't know. It made him profoundly uncomfortable. What was he supposed to say to a complete stranger when they were interrupted constantly by the steps? It was impossible to keep up a conversation of any sort, and he disliked having to answer polite but indifferent questions about himself. This was doubly true now, when he didn't want to reveal anything about his past. He would have to lie when they asked him where he was from, as they would inevitably do, and he abhorred telling lies.

Bingley, however, wasn't taking no for an answer. Sometimes, his friend was like a puppy with a shoe in his mouth, impossible to shake off.

"Why don't you dance with Miss Bennet, if you like her so much?"

"Unfortunately, I have already danced with Miss Bennet twice. I am not allowed to dance with her another time, according to the rules. Who invented those rules, anyway? Do you think, on an informal occasion like this, I could ask her a third time?"

"You know very well that dancing with a young lady more than twice amounts to announcing that you are engaged. I would suppose that it to be true in any ballroom in England, unless things have changed since I left."

"They haven't." Bingley sighed. "Then I will have to content myself with gazing at her."

Darcy suppressed a smile. This was all too familiar. Bingley had always fallen in and out of love with great rapidity. Two weeks from now, he would meet someone else, and Miss Bennet would be forgotten.

"You had better invite some other young ladies to dance. Since you are the newest – and largest – landowner in the district, it will be expected of you. There are several young ladies you haven't danced with yet. I am certain you will find them charming."

"You're right. I am spoilt for choice. I have never seen so many pretty young ladies in one room. Though Miss Bennet outshines them all."

Bingley bounded away happily like a large puppy.

Darcy turned his attention to Miss Bennet, who was standing across the room with her friends and a lady he supposed to be her mother, speaking with animation. Did she really outshine all the young ladies in the room? He would not have called her conventionally beautiful, but her figure was pleasant, and she had a striking liveliness of spirits. The mother had drawn his notice earlier, when they had first entered, since she had shouted to attract Sir William's attention. It was obvious that the mother was a fortune hunter of the most blatant sort. Mrs. Bennet would seize every opportunity she could to ensnare Bingley, he was sure of it.

Elizabeth Bennet, thought Darcy, was dangerous. He had better make certain Bingley did not make a fool of himself over her, and that her mother did not take advantage of his friend's good nature to force him into an impossible situation.

It was a very good thing Darcy had come to Netherfield, after all.

∞ ∞ ∞

Elizabeth Bennet, like any young lady in her position, was offended by Mr. Darcy's dismissal of her looks. No woman liked to be described as merely "tolerable", and Elizabeth was all the more insulted because people generally described her as pretty. To be put down in that manner by a stranger cast doubt on her perception of herself. In the heat of the moment, freshly bruised by the blow, she unwisely recounted what she had overheard to those around her. These happened to be Miss Lucas, her mother and Mrs. Long.

Mrs. Bennet reacted with outrage. "Who does he think he is? First strutting about here and there, then standing against the wall to stare at everyone. He is a nobody – merely Mr. Bingley's impoverished guest. I have a mind to go straight to him and tell him what I think of him, standing there so haughtily and looking down his nose at us!"

Elizabeth shook her head, laughing. By now her chagrin had already disappeared, and she could see how ridiculous the whole thing had been. She wished she had not mentioned the incident. "Now, mama, you know you cannot quarrel with a gentleman simply because he did not like my looks. I do not like Mr. Darcy in the least, so now we are quite equal."

"Quite right, Lizzy," said Lady Lucas. "The best thing we can do is simply ignore him. Besides, he is Mr. Bingley's friend, and we do not want to offend Mr. Bingley, do we, Mrs. Bennet?"

Mrs. Bennet quickly saw the wisdom of Lady Lucas's remark, and made the best of an opportunity to crow a little.

"Yes, one can say anything bad about Mr. Bingley. He is a perfect gentleman. I do believe he is very taken my Lizzy, which is hardly surprising, since she is very pretty, whatever Mr. Darcy's opinion may be. Why, Mr. Bingley danced twice with Lizzy, and seemed very reluctant to leave her side."

Elizabeth was now obliged to accept the congratulations of everyone around her. She objected in vain, saying that Mr. Bingley was merely being polite, but no one listened. Anyone would think Mr. Bingley had already declared himself. As soon as she could, she escaped with her companions.

She could feel Mr. Darcy's gaze on her, but she was determined not to give him the satisfaction of looking at him. No doubt he was looking for her imperfections. Well, let him. His opinion mattered nothing to her, and she fervently hoped she would never have a chance to see him again.

Chapter 5

*N*ews travelled fast, and Mr. Darcy's snub of Miss Bennet was talked of by everyone. The fact that he had not asked any young lady to dance had already turned many people against him, and his insult to Elizabeth clinched everyone's opinion that Mr. Darcy was a churlish gentleman without much to recommend him. The fact that very little was known about him added fuel to the fire. He was universally despised, and even though everyone pronounced him to be a good-looking gentleman, the mysterious Mr. Darcy was judged to be too proud for his own good.

"He did not take the trouble to dance with any of our young ladies. And to snub my Lizzy! Odious man!"

Mrs. Long and Lady Lucas, who were calling at Longbourn, nodded vigorously in agreement.

"Another time, Lizzy," said Mrs. Bennet, "I would not dance with him, if I were you."

Elizabeth chuckled. "I believe, ma'am, I may safely promise you never to dance with him."

"Quite right. Still, you must not mind him, Lizzy. He is of no consequence."

"Mama! I do not mind him in the least. What Mr. Darcy does is of no concern to me at all."

"No concern to you? When he snubbed you in such a manner? So you would sanction his conduct? A penniless young man with nothing to recommend him?"

"If he does not care to be courteous, I am sure that has nothing to do with me. I am very glad he did not dance with me. It spared me the trouble of being polite to him. Besides, I can have nothing to say to someone who does not care to dance."

"*I* do not care to dance," said Mary, stoutly, seeing an opportunity to participate in the conversation.

"Then you and Mr. Darcy share something in common. You're both boring." Lydia swirled one of her ringlets around her finger and began to hum.

"I am *not* boring. Being frivolous doesn't make you less boring. A well-bred lady is never frivolous."

"La! Dancing isn't frivolous," laughed Lydia. "Everyone likes to dance, except you and Mr. Darcy."

An argument ensued, in which Mary said that she could not expect someone as empty-headed as Lydia to understand her dedication to more serious occupations, and Lydia insisted that people who did not enjoy dancing were the dullest type of people in the world.

Elizabeth was glad that the conversation had turned away from her. She would have liked to have forgotten his snub by now, but despite the passage of several days, Mr. Darcy's rejection still rankled, and she resented his high-handed dismissal. The fact that the whole of Meryton felt sorry for her did not improve her feelings towards him.

∞ ∞ ∞

Mr. Bingley, meanwhile, was doing everything right. His fortune was already a high enough recommendation, but in addition, he was gentlemanly and eager to please, and quickly charmed his way into Merton's heart. Consequently, he was invited everywhere, and, determined not to turn down a single invitation, he was frequently seen dining with Meryton's most prominent families.

He had dined once already at Longbourn and had won Mr. Bennet's approval by engaging in sensible conversation over port, and by revealing unabashedly that the origin of his family's fortune was in trade, without either being ashamed or trying to hide it. Mr. Bennet had declared him

When Mr. Bennet and his family met over breakfast the morning after Mr. Bingley's visit, Mr. Bennet made a point of saying that Mr. Bingley was a cheerful young fellow.

"If he offers for you, Lizzy," said her father, "I will happily bestow my blessing, even if I think that, of the two, you are the cleverer. You will have him running around in circles."

"What nonsense you speak, Mr. Bennet! If Lizzy is fortunate enough to receive an offer, she will do all that is proper, and allow him to run her around in circles, or he might change his mind the last moment, and she will be jilted. I hope you will not take one of your father's foolish notions into your head, Lizzy."

"I have no intention of having anyone running around in circles," said Elizabeth, "myself included. Papa, you should know better than to encourage mama in her hopes. She is already implying to everyone who will listen that an engagement is imminent."

Mrs. Bennet looked indignant. "You should listen to your elders, foolish girl! I saw the way he looked at you over dinner. You would be certain the thought has already crossed his mind."

Although Mr. Bingley's attentions went some way to making up for Mr. Darcy's snub, Elizabeth was not quite sure how she felt about it. There was no sign of a thunderbolt yet, and she wasn't convinced that he was serious. It was all very confusing. If she could have willed herself to fall in love with Mr. Bingley, it would have made matters much easier. Fortunately, at this stage she didn't need to decide one way or the other, at least until Mr. Bingley made his intentions clear.

Meanwhile, she was determined to derive as much amusement from the situation as possible, including trying to discover as much as possible about the mysterious Mr. Darcy. She may not like him, but his circumstances piqued her interest. Something didn't quite add up about Mr. Darcy, and she intended to find out what it was.

∞ ∞ ∞

It was two weeks since he had arrived in Netherfield, thought Darcy, and he was desperate in need of reading materials. The owner of Bingley's estate had either taken all his books with him or sold them off, so he was face with empty shelves in beautiful mahogany paneled library. Bingley was not at all bothered by the empty bookshelves. Acquiring books was not a priority for him, nor was it for Miss Bingley, who paid lip service to books but rarely read anything beyond the latest Gothic novel. So, one bright and sunny morning, the Tuesday after the Meryton Assembly, Darcy proposed an outing to see what the Meryton circulating library had to offer. Miss Bingley and her sister expressed great eagerness, and Mr. Bingley looked forward to encountering some of his new friends, so the four of them set out, leaving Mr. Hurst dozing on the chaise-longue.

The circulating library, known as Clarke's, was set up in a spacious Georgian building, and could have accommodated a great many more books, but Mr. Clarke had set it up to please the local readers. The largest section of the bookshop was devoted to Minerva Press publications. It was immediately obvious that it was the focus of the reading public. The area was crowded with a host of young ladies perusing the volumes, whispering and chattering to each other as they compared impressions of the latest sensational novel.

Bingley immediately made himself and his group known to the owner, Mr. Clarke, and asked about the subscription fees. Mr. Clarke, who had never had such distinguished clients, did his best to ingratiate himself by being as pretentious as he could possibly be.

"Our collection is humble," he said to Mr. Bingley, "but we are at your disposal. Any book you require can be ordered for you from London – for an additional subscription, of course. Our local readers are not as fond of the classics or of history as you undoubtedly are, alas! However, I do have several volumes of Greek philosophy upstairs. if you wish to peruse the catalogue, sir, I will fetch them for you."

"Not for me, Mr. Clarke," said Bingley. "I hated the classics at school. I hope never to read one again. However, my friend Mr. Darcy here is more of a scholar. He would undoubtedly be interested."

"I would be interested, too," said Miss Bingley. "I always think there is nothing equal to the classics to improve one's mind."

"I have no interest in the classics at the moment," said Darcy. "I would rather look at irrigation systems."

Miss Bingley would have liked to say she enjoyed irrigation systems, too, but she knew no one would believe it.

She yawned. "I cannot bring myself to be interested in irrigation systems. Matters of business hold no interest for me. However, I admire your dedication and determination to assist Charles with Netherfield, Mr. Darcy."

Darcy did not reply. He turned his attention instead to the catalogue Mr. Clarke had handed him. Miss Bingley hovered next to him for a few more moments, but seeing he was not inclined to speak to her, she grew restless.

"I will see if there is something else that would interest me, though I think it very unlikely in such a limited collection."

Her interest in the classics had waned as quickly as it had appeared, and Darcy noted that she made her way unerringly to the Minerva Press section.

Bingley, meanwhile, had already encountered several acquaintances, and was happily engaged in exchanging pleasantries.

Darcy named a book from the catalogue.

"Where can I find this book?"

"I will fetch it for you, sir."

"If your books are arranged by subject, I would prefer to look at the other books you have as well."

"Certainly, sir."

Mr. Clarke pointed him to a remote corner of the room that was obscured by a column and a bookcase.

"I hope you find something you like, Mr. Darcy."

Darcy hoped so as well, though he did not hold up much hope for it. He had already taken Mr. Clarke's measure, and did not think him a very good judge of the classics. Nevertheless, any book would be better than nothing, which is what he was presently having to contend with at Netherfield.

∞ ∞ ∞

Elizabeth's favorite part of coming to Clark's was not, as one would expect, the opportunity to meet with other acquaintances. She came because she had found a corner where she could read without interruption for an hour or two, which was difficult at Longbourn. Whenever Mrs. Bennet found Elizabeth reading, she would give her something else to do. She did not approve of what she called Elizabeth's bookish inclinations, saying that reading filled a young lady's mind with foolish inclinations. Sometimes, she took refuge in the library with Mr. Bennet, but her father preferred solitude and did not always encourage her to join him.

No one had ever interrupted her in this corner of the library. Her friends knew that she preferred to be left alone. The armchair she sat on, her feet raised on an ottoman, was concealed, and she had come to think of it as her own private space. She was happily reading a volume of essays by Samuel Coleridge when she heard footsteps.

The next moment, Mr. Darcy came around the corner. Startled, and aware of the impropriety of her position, she sat up quickly and rearranged her skirts. The book she was reading fell from her lap to the floor.

"Oh, I beg your pardon, Miss Bennet. I did not mean to startle you."

Mr. Darcy bent down to pick up the book and handed it to her. As she took it, tips of their fingers brushed, and she felt a strange stirring of awareness. She looked towards Mr. Darcy, startled. Their eyes met. He was gazing at her intently. She wondered if he had realized the odd affect he'd had on her. To cover up her confusion, she blurted out the first thing that crossed her mind.

"I do not believe we have been introduced, sir." Then, seized with the spirit of mischief, she added. "You must be new to this town. I do not recall seeing you before. How did you know my name?"

There was a flash of surprise on Darcy's face. She experienced a surge of satisfaction, the sweet taste of vengeance. Take that, Mr. Darcy! He was so accustomed to being noticed he could not conceive that anyone could possibly overlook him.

He recovered quickly, however. "Very true. I apologize for my impropriety. Would you like me to fetch Mr. Bingley and ask him to introduce us?"

Elizabeth did not want to speak to Mr. Bingley at this particular moment, though she could see that her chance of reading in peace was rapidly receding.

"Is Mr. Bingley here? By all means." Then, prompted by the same spirit of mischief, she asked. "How did you know my name, sir?"

He cleared his throat. "I was at the Meryton Assembly."

She willed herself not to laugh. "Indeed? There were many people at the Meryton Assembly. It was quite a crush. However, that does not explain how you know my name."

She enjoyed watching him squirm as he sought for an explanation. He could hardly tell the truth, which was that he had thought her not handsome enough to tempt him. He could also not reveal Mr. Bingley's interest in her. It would be indiscreet.

"Perhaps Sir William happened to offer an introduction."

His hand went to his cravat. Elizabeth reveled in his discomfort.

"I see. And I assume you turned down the opportunity, since I do not recall being introduced."

His fingers tugged at the cravat, seeking to loosen it. "Something must have distracted Sir William."

"Or perhaps you did not wish to be introduced, because then you would have had to dance."

Darcy sent her a searching glance. He was wondering, no doubt, if that was an innocent remark, or if she had in fact overheard him. Well, she was not about to satisfy his curiosity. Let him wonder. She had rattled him. Good. She wanted to. It might be petty of her, but she wanted to bait him, to cause him as much discomfort as he had done to her.

"Since have already been engaged in conversation several minutes without being introduced, perhaps we can dispense with the formality of an official introduction. If you won't tell, I won't, either."

His lips turned upwards, not quite a smile, but something close enough. It would do for now. Elizabeth felt pleased with herself for evoking even that much of a reaction.

He bowed. "Then allow me to introduce myself. I am Mr. John Darcy."

She rose to her feet and curtseyed. "Miss Elizabeth Bennet. Pleased to meet you, Mr. Darcy. Meanwhile, I hope you do not consider it rude if I return to my reading."

"Certainly, Miss Bennet. I am sorry for the intrusion."

She nodded, sat down again, took up her book, and began to read, smiling inwardly.

∞ ∞ ∞

He had been dismissed, thought Darcy, dumbfounded. He was not accustomed to being treated this way. People usually stumbled over each other to talk to him.

Of course, that was when he was Mr. Darcy of Pemberley, not now. He had better grow accustomed to it.

Nevertheless, there something about Miss Elizabeth Bennet that marked her as different from other young ladies he had known. There was a definite trace of laughter in her eyes as she spoke, as though she relished making him uncomfortable. Surely not? He must have imagined it.

He went to the section Mr. Clarke had pointed out examined the books on the shelf, but his gaze kept straying to Miss Bennet. He watched her from the corner of his eye. She was sitting quite still in the armchair, immersed in her reading. What could she be reading that drew her attention so completely, he wondered? Whatever it was, it did not look like a Minerva novel.

He was overcome with a strong urge to ask her but managed to check himself. The conversation had ended. She had made that clear.

He found the book he was looking for, pulled it off the shelf, and looked through it, but he senses were focused on Miss Bennet, and the words blurred on the page.

It was absurd. Why should he not talk to her if he wished to? He snapped the book shut and took a step forward.

She looked up at the noise.

"You seem very immersed in your book, Miss Bennet. What is it you are reading?"

The corner of her lips dimpled provocatively.

"It's a collection of essays by Samuel Coleridge entitled 'The Friend'."

He had known it wasn't a Minerva novel. He felt pleased he had guessed right.

"Are you fond of essays, then, Miss Bennet?"

"Not all essays. I do enjoy Coleridge, however. He has an unusual perspective on things. He is quite the rebel."

He had never read any of the essays when they had first come out in Coleridge's periodical, though he had heard them spoken of. Curious, Mr. Darcy resolved to ask Mr. Clarke for the collection.

"Are you an avid reader, then?"

"Why do you ask, Mr. Darcy? Does it surprise you that we like to read in the countryside?"

Darcy, taken aback by the question, was briefly at a loss how to answer.

"Do you believe us all to be entirely ignorant and provincial?" she persisted.

Was she deliberately challenging him? Her needling tone provoked him to respond, rousing him from his apathy.

"No. On the contrary," he replied. "With all the entertainments available in Town, people have very little time to read. In the countryside, particularly in winter, people have few things to entertain them, so they are more likely to read. As for being ignorant and provincial, ignorance can be found equally in town and country."

She quirked her brow. "I see you are a champion of the countryside. Have you always lived in the country, then, Mr. Darcy?"

Now she was trying to find out more about him. That was not a direction he could let her pursue.

He dodged the question deftly. "Allow me to throw your question back at you. Are you a champion of the countryside? Do you believe it inherently superior to London?"

Her eyes twinkled. "I do not have any prejudice, one way or the other. Human nature is much the same everywhere, I suppose. But you have evaded my question. I will ask it another way. What do you think of Meryton? Do you think it has superior qualities?"

Meryton had pretty young ladies who kept him on his toes. "I suppose if I say I have not spent enough time here to pass judgment, you will say I am evading the question as well."

She tossed back her curls, her eyes dancing. "I will let you off the hook, Mr. Darcy, by asking you an easy question. Why have you come to Clarke's?"

"For the same reason you did. To fetch a book."

"What book is that? I am always eager to know what people are reading. It is a way of knowing which books to read, and which to avoid."

"I suppose you intend to avoid anything I read."

She pressed her lips together to smother a laugh. "Possibly. It depends."

"I can tell you from now, my book is unlikely to appeal to you."

"How can you be so sure?"

"Because it is about agriculture."

Elizabeth laughed. "I was prepared to take offense, but now I must agree with you. I have no interest in agriculture."

She paused as she prepared to strike again. He braced himself for the next question.

"Do you manage your own estate, sir?"

It was as he had expected. This time, he was happy enough to answer. She had provided him with an opportunity to reinforce the story that the Bingleys were circulating about him.

"I manage a small estate in Cornwall, though perhaps the word estate is rather generous, given that the land yields very few crops. It is not mine, in any case."

"So you are a kind of steward, then?"

Every instinct rebelled at being called a steward. His pride cried out for him to deny it, but could not. "I suppose that is a fair description."

She clearly intended to discover more about him. She was perceptive, and would, sooner or later, stumble upon something that would reveal the truth. The wisest course of action would be to discourage her and walk away, but he found himself intrigued her quick mind and impertinent manners. In any case, he did not sense any malice in her. He did not think her curiosity stemmed from a desire to gossip, and there was nothing simpering or false about her. She called a spade, a spade, which appealed to his inherent sense of honesty. It vexed him that he could not be honest with her. He had no choice but to dissemble and conceal the truth.

It would behoove him to throw her off the scent. "Miss Bennet—"

"—Darcy, there you are! I thought I heard your voice. We were planning to leave." Bingley spotted Miss Bennet sitting on the chair. "Miss Bennet! A pleasure to see you here!" He threw Darcy a surprised look. "I see you and Mr. Darcy have become acquainted.

"I happened upon Miss Bennet quite by chance." He sounded more defensive than he had intended. There was something accusing in Bingley's tone.

Meanwhile, Miss Bennet had put down her book and had risen to give Mr. Bingley her hand with a welcoming smile. She had not greeted Darcy that way.

"Are you here to borrow a book as well, Mr. Bingley?"

"Heavens, no. I rarely read. If it is a novel, I am too impatient to know the ending to read it all the way through. I can't help skipping to the end. Then, once I know the ending, I can no longer be bothered to plod through the story itself. If it is a poem, I usually cannot make head or tail of it." He gave a lopsided smile. "I prefer plain English. I do not understand why anyone would labor for so long to create such convoluted rhymes and meanings."

"If I were in your place, Bingley," said Darcy. "I would be ashamed to express such sentiments."

"But you are not in my place, Darcy. I am not embarrassed to speak my mind. I'm a simple fellow and I don't pretend to be otherwise."

"Would you have Mr. Bingley dissemble then, Mr. Darcy?" said Miss Bennet, in a teasing tone. "I think his honesty does him credit."

Darcy raised an eyebrow. "Do you make a virtue of ignorance then, Miss Bennet? If Mr. Bingley had applied himself to his learning better, he could have come to appreciate the fine arts. His careless attitude, however, has always prevented him from applying himself. Do not think to encourage him, Miss Bennet."

"Dash it all, Darcy! I don't see what enjoying poetry has to do with ignorance. I read as much as any other gentleman. I cannot help it if you have nothing better to do than to closet yourself up with books in your library and read all day."

Darcy gave Bingley a warning glance, and Bingley flushed. Bingley had come a little too close to revealing something about Darcy's situation in his eagerness to impress Miss Bennet.

"I am exaggerating, of course, Miss Bennet," said Bingley, hastily. "The fact is, Darcy can sometimes be a little too serious for my taste."

"Is that true, Mr. Darcy? Are you too serious?"

"It depends entirely what Bingley means by the word. If he means to insult me, then he is wide of the mark. There are those who consider me serious. I certainly always taken my duty seriously. Whether that makes me too serious, I have no way of knowing."

"I cannot fault you on that, Mr. Darcy, but I suspect Mr. Bingley meant something else entirely."

"If he is trying to imply that I am gloomy and withdrawn," continued Darcy, "then I cannot be the judge of that. You, Miss Bennet, will have to make your own decision. I give you leave to judge me as harshly as you wish."

She laughed. "You will not trick me into revealing what I think of you, Mr. Darcy, though I do believe anyone who can attend a ball and refuse to dance more than twice in a whole evening could definitely be considered too serious. However, no doubt you will find a way to defend yourself that will shed a different light on the situation."

Ah. She *had* noticed him, after all. She had only implied that she hadn't to annoy him. For some reason, that pleased him.

"No, indeed, I have nothing to say in my defense," he replied, enjoying the novel experience of crossing swords with a lady, "except that I do not like to dance."

"So you think that not liking to dance is enough to excuse you when so many young ladies remained without partners?"

"Well, *I* think it was unforgiveable, Miss Bennet, and I told him so," interceded Bingley, looking from one to the other.

"Then I am to be tried, judged and quartered, simply because I chose not to dance in an Assembly where I knew nobody? Then why do you not consider that I am now making an effort to become acquainted with you, Miss Bennet and intend to do the same with other young ladies? Do you not think I deserve more time, Miss Bennet, before you pass final judgement?"

Miss Bennet laughed. "True enough. I will suspend my judgement, for the moment at least. We will see how you behave at the next ball, if there is to be one."

Bingley was growing restless. He did not like feeling excluded from the conversation. At her words, he brightened. "Miss Bennet, if you wish for a ball, I will be more than happy to hold one at Netherfield," he offered.

She turned her laughing gaze on Bingley. "That is very kind of you, Mr. Bingley, but you must not hold a ball simply to discover whether Mr. Darcy intends to dance or not."

"As for that," Bingley countered, nonchalantly, "I hardly need an excuse for a ball, particularly if it is at your request, Miss Bennet."

He took up Miss Bennet's hand and kissed it.

Darcy felt a tinge of annoyance. Did Bingley have to flirt so openly with Miss Bennet? If her mother had witnessed it, she would be reaching all kinds of conclusions about Bingley's intensions. Even Miss Bennet herself might see it that way.

Miss Bennet, however, confounded Darcy by making nothing at all of Mr. Bingley's gesture. She glanced towards the window and her brow wrinkled.

"Well, Mr. Bingley, I am very glad we ran into each other, but I see there is going to be rain soon. I had better set out on my way. I don't want to be caught in the downpour."

"You needn't worry," said Bingley. "I would be happy to have my driver take you by carriage. I will send for him."

She shook her head. "Thank you, sir, but I prefer to walk. There is nothing quite like a brisk walk in the country, I feel." She curtseyed. "Now you must excuse me."

With that, Miss Bennet took her leave and was out of the door before Darcy could do more than bow.

Once again, Darcy felt disconcerted. He had expected her to push her advantage with Bingley, but she had not. Nor had she shown any interest in lingering to talk to Darcy. Her indifference unsettled him. However, after some consideration, he consoled himself by noting that at least she had not shown a marked preference for his friend.

Chapter 6

wo weeks later, the Bennets were invited to a dinner at Lucas Lodge. Thirty guests had been invited, and the Bennets had been included. Naturally, Mr. Bingley was to be the featured guest.

The Bennets were the first of the guests to arrive at the dinner, thanks to Mrs. Bennet, who wanted to discuss Mr. Bingley's food preferences with Lady Lucas before he arrived. Maria greeted Elizabeth the moment she entered and dragged her into a corner.

"I have bad news, Lizzy. Mama has seated Mr. Bingley next to me. I did everything I could to convince her not to, but she's still hoping he might prefer me over you, all evidence to the contrary."

"You need not apologize, Maria. It's only natural for her to use any opportunity she can to help you."

"I suppose so." Maria scrunched up her nose. "Unfortunately, that's not the worst of it."

What could be worse, in Maria Lucas' opinion? The answer was obvious.

Elizabeth groaned. "Don't tell me. She has seated me next to Mr. Darcy."

Maria nodded. "I asked her not to, but she said there was no other way to arrange the table."

Elizabeth was inclined to think Lady Lucas was being either callous, given that she knew very well that Mr. Darcy had snubbed Elizabeth, or she was exacting her revenge because Elizabeth had stolen Mr. Bingley from her daughter. Well, if she had intended to make Elizabeth feel uncomfortable, she was wide of the mark. Elizabeth thought back to her encounter with Mr. Darcy at Clarke's. She did not particularly like him, but now that she had confronted him, she did not dislike him quite so much. She would not mind locking horns with him again.

"Well, I suppose I shall have to deal with him," she said, cheerfully.

Maria looked relieved. "I'm glad mama hasn't ruined your evening. Perhaps you can even make the best of the situation and find out something more about our mysterious gentleman."

"I shall consider it a challenge, then," said Elizabeth. She resolved then and there that she would not let the evening pass without finding out at least one thing about the mysterious Mr. Darcy.

∞ ∞ ∞

To Elizabeth's delight, Mr. Bingley located her as soon as he came in, and in three swift steps was at her side.

"Miss Bennet. I do hope we are sitting next to each other at dinner."

"I'm afraid we're not. You are too important a guest to sit at my end of the table."

His smile dropped. "It appears I am a victim of my own popularity. I wish I was not. I would much rather spend my time talking to you."

"I am sure we will have an opportunity after dinner."

He perked up. "Yes. We can play cards, or perhaps even dance. Promise you will be my partner at the card table, Miss Bennet."

"I promise," she said, laughing, "but I cannot guarantee I will help you win."

"Oh! I don't care about winning, as long as I can have your company."

Having extracted her promise, he bounded off to join Sir Lucas.

Mr. Darcy entered the house looking withdrawn, and after greeting each of the other guests with a bow and a formal remark, did not utter another word until it was time for the guests to take their seats. He did not approach Elizabeth at all, though she did catch him looking in her direction more than once.

Then, as dinner was announced, and everyone moved to take their places, Lydia came up to Elizabeth and giggled.

"Poor Lizzy! I heard you are stuck with Mr. Silent all evening! Whatever will you do?"

The same thought had been passing through Elizabeth's mind, but she felt compelled to come to Mr. Darcy's defense.

"You should not say such things, Lydia. You don't know anything about him."

Lydia, headstrong as always, refused to be cowed. "Why shouldn't I? It's the truth." Then as Mr. Darcy approached, Lydia gave her a significant look and moved away quickly.

Mr. Darcy stood by gravely as Elizabeth too, took her seat, and the footman pushed in her chair. He bowed to her before he sat down.

"Good evening, Miss Bennet."

"Good evening, Mr. Darcy."

He took up his napkin but said nothing further. She did the same, feeling the awkwardness of her position. She did not want to be the first to speak, because it was up to the gentleman to initiate a conversation. However, even when the footman came by with the soup, he did nothing more than clear his throat.

Well, if he was going to be so uncivil, then she would not talk to him, thought Elizabeth. Let him sit in silence the whole dinner.

Fortunately, the gentleman on her right, Mr. Harris, was much more effusive, and was willing to prattle on to anyone who would listen. At first, she was happy not to endure Mr. Darcy's taciturn presence, but after several meandering accounts, she began to grow restless. Finally, Mr. Harris's attention was drawn away by the lady seated on his other side, and Elizabeth decided to take the plunge with Mr. Darcy.

"Cornwall must be very different from Hertfordshire, Mr. Darcy. I have heard some areas of it are very wild. Is that the case where you live?"

He hesitated for an instant, then answered. "The moors are wild, but much of Cornwall looks like Hertfordshire, with its sheep, fields and hedgerows."

"Do you live close to the sea, Mr. Darcy? Are the cliffs as rugged as they say?"

The corner of Mr. Darcy's lips quirked. "Do you have an interest in geography, Miss Bennet?"

"Perhaps I do. Are you discouraging my curiosity, Mr. Darcy? I am trying to become a little less provincial."

"You are determined to present me as an anti-provincial, whatever you interpret that to be, Miss Bennet. I am not against curiosity. I merely tend to discourage it when it is aimed at me."

Elizabeth was about to retort, but was interrupted by Sir William, who raised his glass to make a toast.

"To our new landowner, Mr. Bingley. I hope we will make you feel very welcome."

Mr. Bingley was basking in the attention, grinning widely. He raised his glass in return. "To many wonderful and lasting friendships."

His gaze wandered around the table and lingered for several moments on Elizabeth. She smiled and raised her glass with everyone else, but heat flooded her cheeks. He ought not to have singled her out from the crowd like that. Had anyone noticed?

As the toast ended and everyone returned to their dinners, she did her best to hide her turmoil by turning all her attention to the venison stew in her plate.

"Is there anything wrong with your stew, Miss Bennet?" said Mr. Darcy. "You look as if you expect something to come walking out of it."

"I certainly hope not," she said, startled into laughter.

"It is very good stew, ma'am, but certainly not worthy of so much curiosity."

There was no doubting the twinkle in his eye. She could not help smiling at him.

"I cannot promise you to refrain from curiosity, Mr. Darcy, but I will hold it back for the time being, if you promise to start another topic of conversation."

Mr. Darcy wiped his mouth on his napkin and prepared to say something, but his neighbor Mrs. Twingly began to talk to him about the owner of Netherfield, Mr. Milbank, and Mr. Darcy was obliged to turn his attention to her.

Meanwhile, Mr. Harris, hearing the name, asked Elizabeth if she remembered Mr. Milbank's dog.

"He was a Great Dane. Big as a horse. Never liked the look of him. What use is a big dog like that?"

"Yes," said Elizabeth, remembering the big dog. "I was terrified of him when I was small. But when I grew older, I found out he was the gentlest creature. I was sad when he died."

"I wasn't," said Mr. Harris. "Good riddance, I say. A dog like that will eat you out of house and home. I don't suppose Mr. Milbank will return to Netherfield again. I heard he is quite the invalid now. He resides in Bath. For the waters, you know. It's good to have healthy young stock at Netherfield."

Elizabeth wondered what Mr. Bingley would think of being called 'young stock'. Would he be amused? She did not know him well enough to judge his reaction. Did he have a sense of the ridiculous? Elizabeth did not think she could marry a gentleman who did not care to laugh.

Sometime later Mr. Harris started to talk politics with one of the gentlemen across the table, and Elizabeth was able to resume her conversation with Mr. Darcy.

"Now, sir, where were we, when we were interrupted?"

"I do believe you were eager to discover the geography of Cornwall. 'Tis a pity we do not have a globe, or I would point out the various towns and villages there."

She chuckled. "Perhaps there is a globe in the nursery. Shall I ask one of the footmen to fetch it?"

Mr. Darcy's lips twitched. "You are incorrigible, Miss Bennet. I do not think it would be considered good manners to do so."

"A pity," she said, her eyes twinkling. "However, since we cannot sit in silence for the rest of dinner, and you have not proposed another subject of conversation, Cornwall is as good a topic as any. Since you did not answer my query about the sea, I will ask you about the moors. Do you walk a great deal on the moors, Mr. Darcy?"

"I am not quite as fond of walking as you are, Miss Bennet, nor do I consider wildness a virtue."

Elizabeth looked down the table to her two sisters, who were laughing and talking loudly. Did Mr. Darcy's statement have a double meaning, she wondered?

"But don't you think there is a wonderful freedom in being alone in a landscape untouched by humans?"

"It is fashionable these days to express enthusiasm about wild landscapes, but I have not yet cultivated that taste. I do not particularly like to "wander lonely as a cloud," as Mr. Wordsworth will have it."

"I take it you like your landscapes tame and civilized, then, Mr. Darcy?"

"I see you disapprove, Miss Bennet, and you might even think me old fashioned."

"I do disapprove," said Elizabeth. "I do not think Nature should be subjected to the whims of people."

"It may be a whim, as you call it, but I confess that I prefer a landscape that produces a good harvest so that the tenants living on the land don't starve. If you deem that a fault, Miss Bennet, then I readily admit to it."

Elizabeth considered his words. Was he speaking about his own tenants, or tenants overall? Was he himself a tenant? His words did not give her enough of a clue.

"Besides," he continued, surprising her by elaborating. "Walking on the moors is not as appealing as you would expect. It is often windy, and the weather changes quickly. There are great mists that rise to swallow you up."

"Surely the moors are not that fearful."

"I prefer to cross the moors, Miss Bennet – if I must -- either by horseback or in the comfort of my carriage if possible. I see nothing appealing in smugglers' inns, highwaymen and horse thieves. I prefer to avoid them whenever possible."

She laughed. "I suppose the moors are not so very different from Hamstead Heath, then, just outside London."

Darcy choked suddenly on a piece of pie and went into such a fit of coughing, he was forced to leave the table.

Elizabeth watched him leave with concern. Should she go and help him? She was of two minds. In the end, she decided she did not want to give anyone – her mother in particular – a chance to call compromise if she and Mr. Darcy were found alone together. Instead, she discreetly asked one of the footmen to tend to Mr. Darcy and hoped that would be enough.

By the time Mr. Darcy returned, the covers were being removed and dinner was coming to an end, so she had no opportunity to inquire about his health as the ladies withdrew.

"Well?" said Maria, as they walked together to the drawing room. "Did you manage to worm any information out of our mysterious Mr. Darcy?"

Elizabeth shook her head. "No. I failed completely."

Despite her failure, however, Elizabeth could not help admiring Mr. Darcy's skill in managing to ward off her questions.

∞ ∞ ∞

The gentlemen did not linger over their port. Not long after, Sir William appeared, with Mr. Bingley at his side.

"Mr. Bingley has had a capital ideal. He has suggested we move the chairs to one side so we can have some dancing." Sir William rubbed his hands together. "We should give the young people a chance to enjoy themselves. Would one of the ladies be kind enough to play some music?"

Miss Bingley immediately put herself forward, shooting a look towards Mr. Darcy, and murmuring that she didn't care to dance with in any case. Mrs. Hurst joined her, ostensibly to turn the pages. However, as they examined the music offered and shuffled it, they began to whisper to each other, and Elizabeth had the feeling that they were making fun of those present.

The moment the music commenced, Mr. Bingley came up to Elizabeth.

"Would you care to dance, Miss Bennet? I particularly like this piccc my aiatcr ia playing."

He had singled her out again. From the corner of her eye, Elizabeth could see her mother looking triumphant and talking to Lady Lucas.

Elizabeth wished her mother would refrain herself a little.

"What a delightful occasion this is, Miss Bennet, is it not?" said Mr. Bingley, as they moved together in the steps of the dance. "I have only been a short time in Meryton, and already I feel I know everyone."

Elizabeth smiled. "That is because you are willing to make the effort to make friends. It is entirely to your credit that you have been embraced by the community."

"Do you think so? But I do not see that I have done anything unusual. People here have been very welcoming, I could not see how I could do otherwise."

Elizabeth seized the opportunity to bring up Mr. Darcy. Perhaps she could discover more about him through his friend.

"Not everyone in your party sees it that way, I am sure. Take Mr. Darcy, for example. He does not seem very happy here."

Mr. Bingley's normally open expression turned cautious.

Elizabeth pressed on. "The two of you seem entirely different, in fact. Have you been acquainted for long?"

Bingley looked relieved. This was a question he could answer. "Oh, yes. Forever. We were at school together."

"But you are younger than he is. How did you become such good friends?"

"That's easy. When I first arrived at Eton I was very shy—"

"—that is hard to believe," Elizabeth interjected.

Mr. Bingley beamed in response. "I'll take that as a compliment, Miss Bennet. But at that point, I was a shy young boy from the north, and had little experience of the type of haughtiness that existed at Eton. I would have been bullied severely, but Darcy took me under his wing when a group of boys were taunting me, and somehow, we hit it off at once. Our friendship has held through the years."

Mr. Bingley had unknowingly given away a crumb of information about Mr. Darcy. Clearly Mr. Darcy was able to hold his own at Eton, which meant that, unlike Mr. Bingley, his money did not come from trade. Elizabeth wondered once again about Mr. Darcy's position in society.

"So what kind of family does Mr. Darcy come from?"

Mr. Bingley's face reddened, and he looked away, avoiding eye contact with Elizabeth. "As you said earlier, Miss Bennet, Mr. Darcy is very private and prefers to keep to himself."

She was even more intrigued. Why was Mr. Darcy at such pains to conceal his past? She wanted to discover more, but she did not want to make Mr. Bingley uncomfortable. Besides, she had the feeling that he would not answer any further questions. She did not wish to provoke Mr. Bingley simply to satisfy her curiosity about a gentleman who didn't concern her. "I'm sorry. I didn't mean to intrude. I was just trying to learn more about your friendship. I am not a gossip, Mr. Bingley."

Part of her questioned that statement. Why was she trying to find out more about Mr. Darcy? Wasn't it because she wanted to be the first to discover Mr. Darcy's past, and to be able to prove that she had worn down his defenses?

Suddenly, she felt ashamed of herself. Since when had she stooped so low? She knew the answer, of course. She was still smarting from his comment at the Assembly.

"I would not reveal any gentleman's secrets, if he did not wish it." She was perfectly serious.

Mr. Bingley brightened. "I never thought you could be a gossip, Miss Bennet, not for a moment, but I hope you don't mind if I don't answer any questions about Mr. Darcy. He is a good friend, and I wish to protect him from speculation."

How very strange! Why did Mr. Bingley think his friend needed protection? Elizabeth looked towards Mr. Darcy, who was standing away from everyone else, looking very ill at ease. His face was shuttered.

"I see. You need not worry, Mr. Bingley. I will not put you in an impossible situation. Your loyalty to your friend does you credit. Come, let us talk of something else."

The tension in Mr. Bingley's shoulders eased.

Elizabeth felt guilty for causing Mr. Bingley discomfort. He did not deserve it. She set her mind on making up to him by giving him her full attention. For the rest of the dance they spoke of other things, and once again, Elizabeth felt so much at ease with Mr. Bingley that it seemed strange to think they had met such a short time ago.

∞ ∞ ∞

Elizabeth was far from suspecting that she was becoming an object of some interest in the eyes of Mr. Bingley's friend. Darcy had at first scarcely considered her to be pretty; he had looked at her without admiration at the ball; and when they next met, he looked at her only to criticize. But no sooner had he made it clear to himself and his friends that she had hardly a good feature in her face, then he began to find it was rendered uncommonly intelligent by the beautiful expression of her dark eyes. He was also forced to acknowledge her figure to be light and pleasing; and in spite of his asserting that her manners were not those of the fashionable world, he was caught by their easy playfulness.

After watching Bingley dancing with Miss Bennet and evidently enjoying himself, he was seized by an unaccustomed desire to do so himself.

When the first dance finished, and Elizabeth moved in their direction, Sir William called out to her.

"My dear Miss Elizabeth, why are not you dancing? Mr. Darcy, you must allow me to present this young lady to you as a very desirable partner. You cannot refuse to dance, I am sure, when so much beauty is before you."

However, to Darcy's surprise, Miss Bennet laughed Sir William's suggestion off. "Indeed, sir, I have not the least intention of dancing. I entreat you not to suppose that I moved this way in order to beg for a partner."

Darcy was by now growing more familiar with Miss Bennet's impertinence, so, rather than taking offence, he said he would be delighted to dance with her and put out his hand to lead her to the dance floor.

"Thank you, Mr. Darcy, but I believe my mother requires my presence."

She walked quietly away, leaving Darcy to follow her movement as she crossed the room. He did not quite know what to make of her rejection. He had never been turned down in a dance by a young lady before. It was a novel experience. He could only conclude it was because she did not know of his fortune.

So this was how it felt not to be Mr. Darcy of Pemberley. It was a bitter pill to swallow.

Chapter 7

*T*wo days later, as the Bennets were taking tea and refreshments, the footman entered with a note addressed to Elizabeth. She took it from the silver salver, surprised. The seal was plain and marked with a B.

Mrs. Bennet's eyes sparkled with pleasure.

"Well, Lizzy, who is it from? What is it about? What does he say? Make haste and tell us."

"Give me a chance to read it, mama."

Breaking the seal, Elizabeth unfolded the note.

My Dear Friend,

If you are not so compassionate as to dine today with Louisa and me, we shall be in danger of hating each other for the rest of our lives, for a whole day's tête-à-tête between two women can never end without a quarrel. Come as soon as you can on the receipt of this. My brother and the gentlemen are invited for cards and we are excluded.

Caroline Bingley

Her immediate reaction upon reading the note was astonishment. When had she become Miss Bingley's 'dear friend'? Why, they had hardly exchanged more than a dozen words! The Bingley sisters must be in an agony of boredom to have invited her.

"Well?" prompted Mrs. Bennet.

"It is from Miss Bingley. I have been invited to dine at Netherfield."

"Just you, Lizzy?"

Elizabeth nodded. Mrs. Bennet squealed with delight.

"I knew it!"

Mr. Bennet looked up from the book he was reading.

"Has Mr. Bingley proposed?"

"You know he has not, Mr. Bennet. But Lizzy has been invited to Netherfield."

"'Tis not what you think, mama. Mr. Bingley and the other gentlemen will not be there."

Elizabeth almost laughed at the disappointment on her mother's face. It did not last long, however. Mrs. Bennet recovered quickly and began to make plans.

"Never mind. We will turn the situation to our advantage. We will contrive to have you stay over. But how?" She stood up and went to the window.

Kitty fell into a fit of coughing, and Mrs. Bennet turned on her irritably.

"Can't you see I am thinking, Kitty? Have you no consideration?"

"I don't cough for my amusement, mama."

"Then do it somewhere else."

The coughing fit ended, and the room became silent, the ticking of the clock a monotonous rhythm in the background, along with a particularly bad piece Mary was practicing in another part of the house. Elizabeth re-read the letter twice and considered whether to accept. She did not relish the idea of spending the evening with the Bingley sisters.

"I have it!" said Mrs. Bennet after several minute's reflection. "You will walk there."

"Walk there? Mama, look at those clouds. It is going to rain."

"Well, of course it is going to rain, silly child. That is the whole point. That way, you will be compelled to stay over."

"That won't work. They will offer to send me home."

"Oh! but the gentlemen will have Mr. Bingley's chaise to go to Meryton; and the Hursts have no horses to theirs, so you cannot return until the gentlemen are back. If they play cards until late, you will have to stay overnight." Mrs. Bennet thought about this some more. "And if you will pretend to be ill—"

"I will not pretend to be ill, and I have too strong a constitution to actually fall ill, so it's no use hoping for it. I had much rather borrow the carriage. Papa, can you spare it?"

Mr. Bennet, who had been following the conversation, surprised her by not coming to her assistance, as she would have expected.

"The carriage is needed on the farm, Lizzy. I'm afraid I cannot."

She shot him an incredulous look. Was he conspiring with her mother?

"There is nothing I can do, Lizzy. If we had known about it yesterday, I would have made other arrangements, but it is currently in use. You can always turn down the invitation and go another day."

Elizabeth nodded. "I think that would be best. If they really wanted to invite me, why could they not have sent a note yesterday?"

"Turn down the invitation!" Mrs. Bennet sputtered indignantly. "Turn down the invitation!" she repeated. "You must be mad. No one turns down an invitation to Netherfield! You will go upstairs and get dressed at once, Miss Elizabeth Bennet. I will hear no more of this nonsense."

Lydia spoke up. "If you do not wish to go, Lizzy, I will go instead. I do believe Mr. Bingley likes me, and with a little encouragement—"

Elizabeth would not put it beyond Lydia to show up at Bingley's doorstep. "Absolutely not! Promise you will do no such a thing."

"I don't see why you must have Mr. Bingley all to yourself. It isn't fair."

"In any case, I will not have Mr. Bingley all to myself," replied Elizabeth, trying her best to be patient but failing miserably. "The ladies are dining alone."

"As mama said, you can always linger. *I* would know what to do."

Elizabeth had no doubt she would.

"Enough," said Mr. Bennet, sounding more stern than usual. "You may be one of the silliest girls in England, Lydia, but you will not embarrass us all by setting your cap at Mr. Bingley. Lizzy, you must go. I will lend you the cart, if you wish. I will have the men unload it."

The thought of arriving at Netherfield riding a common farmhouse cart was preposterous.

"Very well, mama. I will walk. Very likely I will be rained upon," said Elizabeth cheerfully, seeing there was no getting out of it. "If I die of a cold, be it on your head."

"If you do manage to contract a cold, that would be the best possible thing."

Lydia and Kitty giggled. "If you do die, Lizzy, at least it will be for a good reason," said Lydia.

∞ ∞ ∞

Mrs. Bennet had been right about the rain, but if she had known how heavy the downpour would be and what a sorry sight Elizabeth would become, she would not have sent her. It quite defeated the purpose to be so bedraggled that she was virtually unfit to be seen. It was a cold November afternoon, too, and as Lizzy drudged along, the water soaked through her clothing and she grew steadily colder. She would have returned to Longbourn, only she had come so far, and her only desire now was the comfort of a warm room. Since Netherfield could not be more than half a mile away by now, she continued onwards.

It was late afternoon when Netherfield came in sight and though it was not yet dark, the sight of candlelight flickering in the windows was a most welcome sight. The Bingleys would not be stingy about their fires. There would be a big wood fire burning and she would soon be warm again.

As she stood in the doorway, she wondered what would happen if she was refused admittance. Fortunately, the footman who opened the door was a local man, and he recognized her immediately.

"Please step in, Miss Bennet. I know you are expected, but surely you would rather change your clothes first? I will ask the butler, Mr. Sturgeon, what you should do."

When Mr. Sturgeon arrived, he tut-tutted and looked disapproving.

"Surely you did not come here on foot, Miss Bennet?"

"I'm afraid I did."

Elizabeth made light of it, laughing as her sodden clothes and wet hair dripped onto the black and white marble of the hallway.

The severe expression of the butler softened. "Please wait, Miss Bennet. I will send you Mrs. Giddon, our housekeeper. She will deal with the situation."

She was tempted to just show up in the drawing room and shock the Bingley sisters with her uncouth ways, but she didn't know her way around Netherfield, and she knew better than to go pocking her nose into other people's rooms, though she was sorely tempted. In any case, before temptation could get the better of her, Mrs. Giddon appeared.

"Heavens! Look at you, Miss Bennet. We must get you out of those clothes at once, before you catch your death of cold. Please follow me."

Elizabeth, thinking that it was all a big fuss over nothing, followed the housekeeper upstairs.

"If you will slip out of your wet clothes, a maid will fetch you something to wear. You and Mrs. Hurst are of a similar size."

The last thing Elizabeth wanted to do was to borrow Mrs. Hurst's clothes, but she had no choice in the matter. Everything down to her stockings was drenched. She did not care what the Bingley sisters thought of her, but everyone knew that wet clothes were a recipe for contracting a cold, and even with her strong constitution, Elizabeth did not want to risk it.

Besides, she thought, looking in the mirror, she did not want to run into Mr. Bingley with her hair looking like a wet cat's.

∞ ∞ ∞

Armed in Mrs. Hurst's clothes, Elizabeth felt more than equal to joining the Bingley ladies. As she went down the stairs, she saw that Netherfield had undergone a transformation. Elizabeth had been to Netherfield many times, but it had always been a dark, old fashioned place and she had never cared for it. Now it looked completely different. Mr. Bingley had excellent taste. The house looked like an image from the covers of a journal. The furnishings followed the latest trends, and the interior was bright and airy.

Consequently, as she entered the drawing room where the two sisters were waiting, she was able to offer her hostesses a genuine compliment.

"The house looks so much better than it was the last time I was here! It has been beautifully done up."

Miss Bingley looked pleased and gave Elizabeth a sincere smile.

"Then you must really see the Egyptian Room. I have gone to great pains to acquire the pieces it needed. Come with me, Miss Bennet. You will feel yourself transformed to the times of the Pharaohs."

Elizabeth's pleasure in the changes that had been made to Netherfield did not extend to the Egyptian room. It was all the rage, she knew, and she was certain the Bingleys had not spared any expense, but the profusion of colors and the animal feet on all the furniture made the room seem more like an exotic exhibit at a country fair than an actual drawing room. The chairs looked uncomfortable, too, and were more for show than for actual genuine usage. To make matters worse, Miss Bingley spent ages explaining the significance of each piece of furniture and where she had obtained it, so that, by the time they had left, Elizabeth felt exhausted, and the announcement that dinner was served came as a great relief.

∞ ∞ ∞

When dinner was over, and it was time for Elizabeth to leave, she found herself at a loss. Without a way to return home in the dark and rain, as Mrs. Bennet had predicted, Miss Bingley was obliged to offer Elizabeth hospitality for the night.

Elizabeth, meanwhile, would much rather have gone home. Miss Bingley was more gracious as a hostess than as a guest, but Elizabeth had spent more time than she would have liked in her company. The friendship Miss Bingley had claimed existed between them had not blossomed during this period. The conversation had been lively at the beginning but became more strained as the dinner progressed. They all soon discovered they had very little in common and were forced to engage in small talk. Although they were still maintaining a civil conversation, the Bingley sisters seemed to be taking it in turns to yawn, and they were making no effort at all to conceal their boredom.

"Thank you, Miss Bingley," said Elizabeth, responding to the offer of having a chamber made up for her, "but if I may, I would prefer to see if the gentlemen return early. If they do, I can use their carriage to go home."

"We cannot predict when the gentlemen are coming back, Miss Bennet." Mrs. Hurst jingled her bracelets and turned them round and round on her wrist. "You know how it is with gentlemen and cards. They could be at it for hours. We had better have a room prepared, just in case."

A half hour passed, and the yawning increased. Elizabeth began to think it was a bad idea to adhere to her original plan. By now they had all fallen into silence, and since they had nothing more to say to each other, the Bingley sisters were seated at the piano, playing a duet half-heartedly.

Elizabeth was about to confess herself ready to retire when a carriage drew up.

"Ah, my brother is back!" Miss Bingley jumped to her feet, looking relieved.

A few minutes later, Mr. Bingley came running up the stairs and strode into the room.

"The butler told me you were here, Miss Bennet. What a delightful ending to the evening!"

As always, Elizabeth was charmed by his enthusiasm. "Thank you, Mr. Bingley. Unfortunately, I cannot linger. I was about to take my leave. I have been waiting for the carriage to take me home."

"It's pouring cats and dogs outside, Miss Bennet. You can't consider going out at this time of the night, especially in this weather."

Mr. Darcy entered the room at this point and bowed to Elizabeth.

"You are thinking of leaving, Miss Bennet?" He looked grave. "The weather is unpleasant. The wind has picked up. I would not advise going out. In fact, we returned early because of the inclement weather."

That clinched the matter. It would be foolish to make a point of leaving. It would be bordering on rudeness and might imply that she could not endure her hosts' company a moment longer. Besides, she had already suffered a soaking. She wasn't eager to face the elements again, in a cold and rattling carriage buffeted by the wind.

"If you do not advise it, Mr. Darcy, then I will take your advice, along with Mr. Bingley's." She turned to her hostesses. "Thank you. I accept your invitation."

"And you must plan to stay for dinner tomorrow as well," said Mr. Bingley.

Elizabeth did not know what to say. She did not enjoy the company of either Mr. Darcy or the Bingley sisters, but Mr. Bingley's sunny smile won her over. It would be an opportunity to know him better and to see him in his own home. It might also help her to determine if his interest in her was serious.

"Thank you, Mr. Bingley. I will send a note to my parents in the morning to let them know I will be delayed."

The blazing smile he gave her was more than enough reward.

∞ ∞ ∞

The next day, Elizabeth woke up with a headache. She ignored it, assuming it would go away as the day progressed, but it did not. As they sat down at dinner, she began to feel lightheaded as well, and she started to wish she could go upstairs and lie down.

At first, no one commented on her uncharacteristic silence. Both Mr. Bingley and Mr. Darcy sent some questioning looks her way, but she countered them by making more of an effort to contribute. She did not want to give Mr. Bingley a bad impression of her socializing skills. However, she soon found it too fatiguing to maintain a conversation and wondered if she should excuse herself and go home.

"You look flushed, Miss Bennet." Miss Bingley and Mrs. Hurst exchanged knowing smiles. "Perhaps the wine was too strong for you?"

"Very likely." By now Elizabeth was feeling quite faint. "I must excuse myself. It is quite late. If you will be so kind as to have the carriage brought round, I can return home."

"But it is only seven o'clock. Surely you don't keep such unfashionably early hours here in Meryton?" There was a sneer on Miss Bingley's face.

"I daresay we do." Elizabeth heard Miss Bingley's quiet malice from a great distance. What was wrong with her? It was almost as if someone had given her a sleeping potion. She was unaccountably drowsy. She had better leave quickly before she made a fool of herself.

She turned in Mr. Bingley's direction. "I need my carriage, Mr. Bingley."

"Of course." He gave orders to one of the footmen.

The carriage took ages to arrive. Elizabeth, meanwhile, was conscious that she was disturbing their dinner. They were too polite to eat until she left, and the dishes on the table were turning cold.

Finally, the footman came to announce that the carriage was waiting. Elizabeth stood up quickly, but a strange giddiness overtook her and, swaying, she was forced to cling to the side of the table.

"See to the lady," said Darcy, throwing down his napkin and coming quickly to her side. He took hold of her elbow to steady her.

"I am perfectly well, Mr. Darcy," She pulled away.

She was aware of Miss Bingley watching, no doubt assuming that she was doing this to attract attention.

"Miss Bennet, you are mistaken in the matter. You are not well at all. You cannot leave."

"I assure you, Mr. Darcy, I am capable of walking down the stairs and out of the door—"

She took a few steps forward, but her legs betrayed her. They were alarmingly weak, and the room spun around her. She felt a steadying hand take hold of hers. It was Mr. Darcy again.

"You are burning up with fever, Miss Bennet, I can feel it through your glove. You cannot leave the house. I insist that you stay."

She bristled at Mr. Darcy's commanding manner. She would not allow him to make decisions for her

"But—."

Mr. Bingley was at her side now, looking at her kindly. "If you have a fever, Miss Bennet, you cannot go out in the damp. It would be far better for you to rest. I will send a servant to fetch the apothecary"

His gentle tone was Elizabeth's undoing. She could not say no to Mr. Bingley.

She nodded. He smiled and put out the crook of his elbow.

"Come. Lean on me. I will help you upstairs. Louisa, can you take the other side, please?"

"This way, Miss Bennet." Louisa clutched her other arm.

On her way to the door, Elizabeth passed Mr. Darcy, who was looking grave. He probably thought she had deliberately made herself ill. She felt compelled to explain the matter to him.

"I have a strong constitution, Mr. Darcy," she pointed out. "I never get sick."

The corner of his mouth quirked. "All the more reason to take care of yourself so you can recover."

He bowed. She wanted to curtsey back, but her legs felt too weak, so she waved to him instead and tried to move in as dignified a manner as she could out of the room and up to the bedchamber, where a maid was warming the bed for her with a bedpan of coals.

Mrs. Hurst and Mr. Bingley withdrew, wishing her a quick recovery. The maid helped her undress and get into bed. The pillows were wonderfully soft. They felt cool against her cheek. Elizabeth sank into them and began to drift into sleep almost immediately.

The last thought she had, was that her mother had won after all. Elizabeth had been forced to stay another night at Netherfield.

Chapter 8

*I*t cannot be said that Elizabeth was entirely neglected by her family during her illness. On the third morning, Mrs. Bennet arrived, accompanied by her daughters and full of advice about how Elizbeth was to be cared for. Upon her arrival, Mrs. Bennet hurried straight upstairs to look in on Elizabeth, her anxiety evident in the way she crushed her handkerchief and held it to her mouth.

"You had better stay down here, girls."

As it would not do for the young ladies to be kept waiting at the bottom of the stairs, Mr. Bingley invited the Bennet sisters to the drawing room, where his two sisters were already seated.

Lydia, who had come to Netherfield with a specific purpose, looked around her as she entered.

"This is a prodigiously large drawing room. It is big enough to double as a ballroom." She immediately turned to Mr. Bingley. "You know, Mr. Bingley, the last time we met, you said you intended to hold a dance. When Lizzy is better, we will hold you to that promise, for there is nothing like a dance to cheer everyone's spirits in winter."

Miss Bingley looked disgusted, but Mr. Bingley smiled and declared that it was a splendid idea, and that he would start planning it the moment Miss Bennet was well enough to emerge from the sickroom.

Lydia was so pleased with the outcome of her enquiry that she actually stirred herself to be polite to the Bingleys by engaging in small talk.

A few minutes later, Mrs. Bennet came down the stairs and joined them, looking cheerful.

"I was so overcome with anxiety when I received your note informing me of Lizzy's illness, Mr. Bingley, I have not slept a wink since. Only the knowledge that you have sent for the best apothecary around, and that she is receiving even better care than she would have at home, prevented me from rushing over to be at her bedside. I really must thank you for ensuring she was nursed back to health, for you never know with a cold." She shuddered. "Thank heavens it wasn't any more serious."

"I echo that sentiment, Mrs. Bennet," said Mr. Bingley. "Luckily, Miss Bennet has a strong constitution."

"Oh, she has the best constitution in the world. Lizzy is never ill." Then, remembering that Elizabeth *was* ill on this particular occasion she added. "However, if she does fall ill, it never lasts." Then, afraid that she would be expected to take Elizabeth home immediately with her, she added, "However, I do not think she is quite well enough to be moved just yet. It might risk a relapse. It is just that I do not wish to cause you any more inconvenience. We have imposed on your hospitality long enough."

"You must not dream of exposing Miss Bennet to the cold at this point, ma'am. Miss Bennet must stay as long as necessary for her to recover fully. I am more than happy to help in any way I can."

Mr. Darcy and Mr. Hurst came in at that moment. Mr. Darcy looked startled to see Mrs. Bennet there with her daughters. However, he bowed politely and enquired after Elizabeth's health.

Mrs. Bennet replied briefly that Miss Bennet was much improved.

"I am glad to hear it."

Since Miss Bingley did not offer the Bennets refreshments, they were obliged to leave soon after. As they drove away, Mrs. Bennet remarked.

"Did you hear what Mr. Darcy said? He said he was glad to hear Lizzy was better, as if he wishes to be rid of her as soon as possible."

"Never mind Mr. Darcy, mama. I persuaded Mr. Bingley to have a ball when Lizzy recovers."

"You are a clever girl, Lydia. Lizzy had better get well quickly. If I had known about the ball, I would have told her to come home at once. I will send the carriage round for her tomorrow."

∞ ∞ ∞

If Mr. Bingley was surprised the next morning to find Mrs. Bennet calling on them again so soon, he did not show it. Mrs. Bennet declared she was impatient to have her dear daughter home and could not be without her for another day. This sudden change of sentiment seemed to him entirely natural, and he took it to be a mother's concern for her daughter. He was not happy about it. He had been looking forward to spending some time with Miss Bennet, but it was not to be, and he could not object without revealing too much of his own feelings.

Miss Bennet was already much improved in any case, and had joined them briefly in a game of cards in the library the evening before.

As for Miss Bingley, she was gratified that Miss Bennet was leaving, since both her brother and Mr. Darcy were making too much of a fuss over what Caroline thought of as a trivial cold.

Mr. Darcy was startled by the news of Miss Bennet's unexpected early departure and experienced a much stronger feeling of disappointment than he would have expected. He had grown accustomed to having her under the same roof, and the thought that her bedchamber would now be vacant left him with a feeling of emptiness. He hovered as she said her goodbyes and followed her out to the carriage. As she was about to get in, he held her back by asking her whether she had enough books to occupy her while she was recovering.

"Thank you, Mr. Darcy, I think I do."

But he did not want her to go empty-handed. He wanted her to take something of his with her, something that would remind her of him.

"If you will wait just one moment, I believe I have something you will enjoy."

He ran upstairs to bring her a copy of a book he had recently acquired. It was entitled, "The Landscape of Hertfordshire, with Scenic Walks."

He hurried out to find Miss Bennet already seated inside the carriage, which was about to leave.

Elizabeth pulled down the window as he approached.

"I do believe you will like this, Miss Bennet, considering your interest in geography."

She smiled, remembering their conversation. "Why, thank you Mr. Darcy. However, it was the geography of Cornwall that interested me."

He smiled back. "I am not yet convinced of that. We will have to discuss the matter further."

Mrs. Bennet, who was starting to fidget, leaned over.

"Thank you, Mr. Darcy, but we must take our leave. I do not wish Lizzy to be exposed to the cold for too long."

"Of course." He immediately felt guilty for his lack of consideration.

He bowed and stood back quickly to allow the carriage to move away, then followed it with his gaze until it became no more than a dot on the horizon.

∞ ∞ ∞

The carriage had hardly moved when Mrs. Bennet decided to issue a warning.

"You shouldn't waste time talking to Mr. Darcy, Lizzy. Lady Lucas says he doesn't have a penny to his name and is looking to find an heiress who will revive his fortunes."

Elizabeth swiftly pulled up the window, praying that Mr. Darcy had not overheard her mother's remarks.

"Hush, mama. Do not say such things. You never know who will overhear."

"Oh, I care nothing for the opinion of Mr. Darcy."

"But he is a friend of Mr. Bingley's, and I will see him regularly if I marry Mr. Bingley."

"If you are married to Mr. Bingley, it will not matter one fig what Mr. Darcy thinks of you. You will have everything you need. Mr. Darcy will not signify."

"He will signify to me, mama," said Elizabeth firmly, "As my husband's friend. I wish you would be polite to him."

"Why, Lizzy, one could almost think you have formed an attachment to Mr. Darcy. I hope not. It will not do at all."

Her mother's conclusion shocked her. "You are entirely wrong, I assure you. I have not formed an attachment for Mr. Darcy. I dislike the man."

She puzzled over her mother's remark several times during the course of the day. It was preposterous, of course, and she was able to dismiss it after giving it careful and rational consideration. Still, the idea niggled at her, and later, in the middle of the night, Elizabeth found herself awake, wondering how Mrs. Bennet could possibly have jumped to such a conclusion. Elizabeth had no interest at all in Mr. Darcy. As Mr. Darcy himself was well aware, she was merely curious to find out more about him. He was a mystery, and that was why he interested her.

But as she drifted into the world of dreams, his tousled hair and honey brown eyes appeared before her, with lips that were curling into a small smile. There was tenderness in his eyes, and she felt a little lurch in her stomach as he looked at her.

It was the last image she saw before she crossed over into sleep.

∞ ∞ ∞

Four days later, Mr. Bingley called at Longbourn with his sisters to issue an invitation. The Netherfield ball was to be held Tuesday of the next week. Needless to say, Mrs. Bennet let it be known among all their acquaintances that Mr. Bingley had come in person to invite Elizabeth, thus confirming to everyone that the ball was being held especially for her daughter.

Meanwhile, it seemed the invitation was a signal for the rain to start up again, because it rained every single day. Elizabeth thought she would go mad. She was unable to go for her usual walks, and, cooped up in the house, was forced to endure Kitty and Lydia's constant moaning about not being able to go to Meryton for the latest gossip, as well as Mary's wretched piano rehearsals in anticipation of performing at the ball.

"Now, Lizzy, you know Mr. Bingley has set up this ball for your sake. He has gone to a great deal of trouble for you. You had better not ruin everything by being obstinate. Mr. Bingley has an income of five thousand a year. You will be comfortable for life, with as many new gowns and carriages and servants at your beck and call as you could dream of. Think, Lizzy, and don't let that tongue of yours get the better of you. You have happiness within your grasp. Don't ruin it all."

Elizabeth sighed. "What makes you so certain that Mr. Bingley is sincerely attached to me? I know he admires me, but I confess I don't see any evidence of an enduring passion."

"You don't need an enduring passion, child. You just need him to feel he wants to marry you. Afterwards, when you know each other better, you will develop a different type of affection. Look at me and Mr. Bennet, for example."

Elizabeth would have liked to point out that there was no affection between mama and Mr. Bennet, but if mama chose to believe that it existed, who was she to cast doubt on it? It was hardly her concern in any case. She was much more interested in sorting out her thoughts about Mr. Bingley.

"I am not entirely convinced we will suit."

"Not suit? And what has that go to do with anything?" Mrs. Bennet dropped her sewing to the floor and took out her handkerchief from her sleeve. The kerchief fluttered back and forth like a flag as she waved it about. "You will be the death of me one of these days. Oh! My poor nerves!" She blew her nose loudly.

"Look what you have done now, Lizzy." Lydia looked daggers at her sister. "Mama, don't listen to a word she's saying. You know she is only funning. Aren't you, Lizzy?"

Elizabeth remained silent.

"Surely you are not so stupid as to turn down Mr. Bingley, Lizzy, particularly after he has gone to the trouble of throwing a ball for you?" Mrs. Bennet was so flustered now, she began mop her brow with the handkerchief. "I warn you, Miss Elizabeth Bennet, if you refuse Mr. Bingley, I will turn you out on the streets to fend for yourself!"

Had Mr. Bingley really thrown the ball in her honor, or was it simply his way of announcing his arrival to the vicinity? Elizabeth had gone over every detail of her stay at Netherfield to determine Mr. Bingley's feelings towards her. She had been ill, and they had not spent much time together, so it was difficult to determine the extent of his attachment. He had certainly seemed solicitous, yet Mr. Darcy had been equally solicitous. It proved nothing more than that they were both thoughtful and courteous gentlemen.

As for how she felt about Mr. Bingley, she could undoubtedly say she liked him very much indeed. It was impossible not to like Mr. Bingley. He was kind, impeccably dressed, handsome and charming. Much more to the point, did she truly want to spend the rest of her life with him?

Her mind answered yes. To be the mistress of an estate like Netherfield! It was surely every woman's desire. How could she possibly say no to such a prospect? To be able to spend part of the year in Town, to attend fashionable gatherings and wear the latest fashions?

There was another reason to marry Mr. Bingley. It was petty, she knew, but Elizabeth wanted to thumb her nose at Mr. Collins. He had warned her, when she turned down his proposal, that she may never have such an opportunity again. It would be delightful to prove him wrong.

Yes, she was prepared to spend the rest of her life with Mr. Bingley.

Yet at the same time, her heart revolted. Could she really be satisfied with a loveless marriage? What would she talk with him over breakfast? Over dinner? Then there was the matter of his sisters. She could not imagine living with them under the same roof for weeks at a time. She supposed Miss Bingley would eventually marry and spend less time with Mr. Bingley, but what if she didn't?

"You know Lizzy doesn't mean half the things she says, mama. You need not take it so hard. La! Do stop being foolish, Lizzy. Of course you're going to marry Mr. Bingley! Then we can all go to Town. We will attend balls and dances and go to Vauxhall. What fun we'll all have!"

"We can even go to masquerade balls!" Kitty and Lydia looked at each other and giggled.

Mr. Bennet entered the room at that moment, and, shaking his head, remarked, as he always did, that Kitty and Lydia were the silliest young ladies in England.

"They are not the silliest," remarked Mrs. Bennet, with emphasis. "It is Lizzy who has no sense at all. Imagine, she means to refuse Mr. Bingley!"

"Oh? And has Mr. Bingley asked for her hand in marriage? If so, I confess myself deceived in him. I thought he was more of a gentleman. He ought to have consulted me in the matter. Tell him he must ask my permission, Lizzy. It is customary to do so."

"Oh, how you love to tease me, Mr. Bennet! Of course he has not. But he will, mark my words."

"Well, then." Mr. Bennet fixed his gaze on Elizabeth. "Do you intend to turn him down, Lizzy?"

"I have not yet made up my mind."

"Since nothing has happened yet, and no decision has been reached, I suggest we postpone this discussion, Mrs. Bennet, until there is good reason to have it."

"But by then it will be too late!" wailed Mrs. Bennet.

"Now, now, my dear, you must not become so agitated. It is not good for your nerves, you know. Chances are he will not propose, and then it will all have been for nothing."

With that he left the room, leaving Mrs. Bennet muttering darkly that gentlemen had no understanding of these things and should not intervene when they knew absolutely nothing.

Elizabeth took advantage of her mother's distraction to escape to her bedchamber, unwilling to continue a conversation that was doomed to lead nowhere.

Chapter 9

The day before the Netherfield Ball, the unexpected happened. Mr. Bennet, who had been feeling under the weather for a few days, was taken violently ill with a raging fever. When the apothecary was summoned, the dreaded verdict was received. The prognosis was not good. It was a putrid sore throat, and a virulent one. The apothecary bled his patient and prescribed a tonic, but he did not hold out much hope. The next two days, he said, would decide whether the patient would continue to decline or whether there would be a turning point.

Mrs. Bennet succumbed to a violent attack of the nerves. Convinced that Mr. Bennet was on his deathbed, she trembled in fear that Mr. Collins would arrive any minute to take over Longbourn. Nothing could persuade her otherwise.

"For you can be sure of it. If the servants know, everyone will know, and I would not put it past Lady Lucas to send an express to Charlotte to tell her to prepare to take her place here."

In the end, she had to be given laudanum to calm her, and Elizabeth made way for her mother to sleep in her room while Elizabeth sat up at her father's side, alert to every movement he made. His fever was high, and he was delirious. She had never seen him so ill, and her anxiety increased by the hour. She tried to distract herself with the book Mr. Darcy had given her, but she barely knew what she was reading. Her mind and emotions were in such an upheaval, she barely remained seated. Several times, she jumped up and walked about the room, but nothing seemed to help.

As her father's condition worsened, Elizabeth was struck forcibly with the reality of Mrs. Bennet's fears. The arrival of her cousin Mr. Collins with Charlotte no longer belonged to some obscure future she could barely envision. She could imagine it all too well now. She could see how it would be.

The ladies of Longbourn would be tolerated for a week or two, but they would soon be degraded to the position of guests, and they would feel like intruders in their own home. They would be reminded constantly that they were dependent on the charity and goodness of Mr. Collins. Eventually, they would be made to feel unwelcome, no matter how much Charlotte would try to conceal it. Only now did Elizabeth realize how close they were to destitution. Everything depended on her father's health. If it gave way, they would be left with nothing.

Too late, she understood that her indolence in the matter of marriage would cost them dearly. Too late, she wished they had made more of an effort to plan for this eventuality, to put aside something that would tide them through. Where were they to go? Uncle Gardiner would welcome them, of course, but with so many children there was very little room for all of them. She, perhaps, could stay with Jane, but for how long?

A grim future stretched before her.

Mr. Bennet groaned and, lifting his head, put out his hand to her.

"Is that you, Lizzy?"

She went to him quickly, her heart beating in hope that the fever had broken and he had become lucid again.

"Mr. Collins is a fool. You mustn't marry him, no matter what your mother says." He grasped her hand urgently.

Her heart sank. He did not know what he was saying. "Hush, papa. Don't trouble yourself on this matter. I promise you I will not marry Mr. Collins."

He sank back into the bed, reassured, and in an instant, Elizabeth was forgotten. She held onto his hand for a moment longer, but he pulled it away peevishly and tossed about.

When the next day dawned, his condition remained the same. Elizabeth, who was stiff from her vigil, called for Mrs. Hill to replace her, and went down to fetch herself something to eat. To her astonishment, she found her sisters still engaged in preparing for the Netherfield Ball.

"What does this mean?" she cried. "How can you think of a ball at a time like this?"

"There is nothing I can do for papa," said Lydia, sullenly. "I cannot make him better by staying behind. You can remain here and nurse him, Lizzy, but I have been looking forward to the ball for weeks, and I will not give it up merely because papa is ill."

Elizabeth had a great deal to say to that, but she did not have the strength to argue after a sleepless, anxious night. She left the room, determined to address the question at a later time. Whether her sisters chose to go was up to them and their conscience. However, one thing was abundantly clear to her. There was no chance of her going to the Netherfield Ball. Wild horses would not drag her there.

∞ ∞ ∞

Mr. Darcy had been more affected by Miss Bennet's stay at Netherfield than he had expected. Even though they had hardly spoken, her mere presence in the same house had woven her into his life. He admired her independent spirit. Even when she was unwell, she did not like to ask for help or acknowledge any weakness. She was refreshingly free of feminine wiles. She could have taken advantage of her illness to demand attention, but she did not. There was a no-nonsense manner about her that he found appealing.

Yet, despite the fact that she had made no effort at all to capture his attention, he found his thoughts drifting towards her far more often than they ought to. He tried to suppress them, but they eluded his control.

At first, he worried about this. It was out of the question to allow himself any entanglements in his present circumstances. He had made a point of steering clear of anything but the most fleeting and insignificant flirtations when he was an officer, and since his return to England, he had practiced the most severe restraint. Yet here he was, in little more than a month, paying more attention than he should to a young country miss who had made no effort at all to draw his interest. She had somehow managed to captivate him with her vivacious manners and easy conversation, to say nothing of her expressive eyes.

The truth was, he had been unhappy for so long, lost in his own private darkness, that Miss Bennet's laughter and lightness drew him like a beacon of hope. He told himself there was no harm in pursuing an acquaintance that had come about in full view of all the inhabitants of Meryton. Surely he deserved a little reprieve from the nightmare that had haunted him for three years?

Having assured himself that his interest in Miss Bennet was limited to a need for friendship and companionship, he allowed himself to daydream, just a little. He was particularly looking forward to seeing her at Netherfield again. This time, he decided, he would dance with her not once, but twice.

∞ ∞ ∞

The day of the Netherfield Ball arrived, and Mr. Darcy's spirits were remarkably high, considering he did not like to dance. He came down to breakfast with a light step, and found Bingley already at the table, looking even more cheerful than usual.

"Darcy! I am in a fever of impatience. I cannot wait for the evening to begin."

"We should go for a long ride. That will take up some of the time, if you are really so impatient. I see you are enjoying the feeling of being a landowner in the country."

"More than I imagined. I like to be among people I know. In Town, you are always surrounded by strangers. However, that is not the only reason I am looking forward to tonight." He paused. "I'm sure you know the main reason."

Darcy raised his brow. "I am certain you are about to tell me."

"It is Miss Bennet, of course!"

The name brought up such a flood of emotions in Darcy that he did not initially pay much attention to what Bingley was saying.

"—a perfect angel. I have never seen a young lady so perfect. Do you not think so, Darcy?"

Darcy was accustomed to effusions of this sort from Bingley. He had known Bingley since he was very young and had heard those same words from him on numerous occasions. This time, however, the words had a distasteful effect on Darcy, who wished his friend did not apply the same words to Miss Bennet as he had applied to others.

"You cannot expect me to take you seriously, Bingley. You said the same thing about Miss Gillmore, and about Miss Hewitt before her, and in your letters, you called Miss James an angel as well."

"This is different, Darcy. Miss Bennet is like no other woman I have met."

Darcy found himself more impatient with his friend than he had ever been. "It is always different. Every single time. I am tired of hearing it. Miss Bennet does not deserve to be treated like one of your flirtations. I will not sit here and listen to her name bandied about in this manner."

Bingley stared. "All I said was that she was an angel. I don't know what's come over you, Darcy. It is not as if I am insulting her. I have the utmost respect for Miss Bennet."

"Then kindly refrain from speaking about her at all," said Darcy. "I do not wish to hear any more of your impulsive sentiments."

At that, Darcy stood up, threw down his napkin, and left the room. As he left, he ran into Miss Bingley, who was looking very flustered.

"I wish Charles had thought to consult me before agreeing to have this ball. When you live in a provincial village, you cannot expect to have all the amenities you have in London. I am tearing my hair out trying to obtain some of the basic things we take for granted in Town. For example—"

Darcy had no wish to hear a list of all the things Miss Bingley was unable to obtain. However, her criticism of her brother found a ready recipient.

"Bingley is a selfish, inconsiderate young man. I am in complete agreement with you, Miss Bingley. He never thinks beyond the moment. One day, he is going to find himself in trouble."

Miss Bingley was taken aback by the emphatic manner in which Mr. Darcy issued this statement, but since he was agreeing with her, she could not very well fault it. Pleased to find someone to whom she could confide her grievances, she immediately launched into an attack on her brother.

Mr. Darcy, having vented some of his ire at his friend, listened politely for a few minutes, then excused himself and retired to the library, where he sat down to write a letter to his sister.

Dear Georgiana,

I have fled to the library where I can be away from the frantic preparations for the ball this evening. Bingley has invited everyone of any consequence within five miles, and it promises to be what fashionable people call 'a crush'. Miss Bingley is in a whirl of activity. I cannot understand how ladies can find enjoyment in organizing such an event. It is completely exhausting and involves so many details I want nothing more than retreat into peace and quiet until it is all over. Miss Bingley is an exacting employer. I pity the poor servants who live in fear of being reprimanded whenever she enters a room. Meanwhile, Bingley has thrown himself into the preparations with his usual zeal. He also has the unenviable task of soothing Miss Bingley whenever something goes wrong. I have been at the receiving end of Miss Bingley's complaints myself. However, I managed to extricate myself as quickly and as painlessly as possible.

Speaking of Bingley, he once again believes himself in love. This time, it is with Miss Bennet. Have I told you about Miss Bennet? I may have mentioned that she stayed here at Netherfield when she was ill. She is an animated young lady who is inclined to speak her own mind and to find something to laugh at in every situation. She has a pair of expressive dark eyes and a fine figure. Unfortunately, she puts herself forward too much. I have not quite made up my mind whether I approve of her. Nevertheless, I must acknowledge that she is one of the handsomest ladies of my acquaintance.

Bingley is besotted with Miss Bennet, but I do not believe they would suit at all. If Bingley is to improve his status in society, he needs to marry someone of more consequence than a country gentleman's daughter. Her family shows a definite lack of breeding. Her sisters run wild and her mother's family is in trade. I am convinced that such a match will be harmful to his social standing and will significantly reduce the chances of his sister Caroline marrying well. They have made such an effort to distance themselves from their undesirable background; it would be a pity to destroy all they have worked for in a moment of folly. We are all hoping that Bingley's attachment to Miss Bennet will fizzle away as quickly as it started. He has often declared himself violently in love, only to lose interest a week later when someone else captures his attention, so it is very likely to be the case in this situation as well.

I see that I have filled two sides of the letter already, and must therefore write the rest cross-lined, which I dislike, because it destroys the neatness of the writing. I will tell you more next time. I am certain you will want to hear some details about the ball, what the ladies wore, etc. I will do my best to oblige, though you must remember that I am hardly an expert in feminine fashion and fripperies.

Your affectionate brother William

Chapter 10

*J*n the afternoon, Mrs. Bennet rose from her bed, the effect of the laudanum having worn off. She came immediately in search of Elizabeth, who was once again at her father's bedside.

"What are you doing here, Lizzy? You must go and get ready for the ball at once!"

"I will not go to the Netherfield ball, mama, not when papa is so poorly. *You* have to go as a chaperone for the others, of course, but I will stay behind and look after him. If his condition worsens, I will send for you."

"He is not as bad as all that," said Mrs. Bennet. "I can see he is already improved since yesterday."

Elizabeth had not seen any improvement at all, but she kept her thoughts to herself. "Nevertheless, he is very ill, mama."

Mr. Bennet, perhaps overhearing, perhaps reacting to something in his feverish mind, grew agitated.

"'Tis nothing," he said.

Elizabeth immediately set out to reassure him. "Of course, papa. You will be better in no time, I'm sure, especially with me to nurse you back to health."

Mrs. Bennet protested. "You will not—"

Elizabeth put her hand to her lips and indicated the door, pulling her mother's sleeve. Mrs. Bennet sighed and followed her daughter as she left the room and shut the door behind her.

"Really, mama. Must you upset papa when he is so very ill?"

"You exaggerate, child. He will make a full recovery and be out of bed by tomorrow."

Elizabeth did not voice her concerns. She did not want to alarm her mother again and have her fall into another fit. "The point is, until I am certain, I cannot dance and frolic, knowing papa is alone and suffering."

"You have no choice, Lizzy. Mr. Bingley is expecting you."

Elizabeth pressed her lips together. Anyone who knew her well enough would have recognized that obstinate look. She had no intention of backing down. "I would not go, even if the Prince Regent himself were to order me to do so."

Mrs. Bennet glared. "You are a selfish, spoilt girl, Lizzy Bennet. I will not indulge your every whim. You *cannot* be whimsical like your father. Look where that got us." She lowered her voice to a harsh whisper. "We are only a step away from destitution, you horrid child. If your father is carried away, what do you think will become of us? Your clever friend Charlotte will be happy enough to see us out of this house. You cannot expect mercy from her. She and her husband will turn us out within a fortnight, particularly since you insulted Mr. Collins by refusing his proposal."

"Kindly refrain from speaking about my friend in this manner, mama." Elizabeth spoke coldly, but she knew Mrs. Bennet was right. She had already come to that conclusion last night. It pained her to be thinking this way. It seemed so mercenary, but it was also natural to fear for their future.

Mrs. Bennet, sensing Elizabeth's uncertainty, pressed on. "If we are homeless, your chance of contracting a decent marriage will be finished, and you will be forced to live as spinster at your uncle's house. Is that how you wish to spend the rest of your days?"

"All the more reason to stay at papa's bedside and nurse him to health."

"Are you an apothecary? Do you have some special knowledge of herbs? You can be no use to anyone sitting and staring at your father all evening. You cannot help him. But you can help *us*. You are the only one that stands between us and impoverishment."

Why must it be like this? Why were the choices of women so limited? Why must she marry to secure the family's future? Everything in her rejected the idea, but the reality was stark.

Knowing now that Elizabeth was almost convinced, Mrs. Bennet pressed on. "You must fix Mr. Bingley's interest immediately. It is your duty to marry Mr. Bingley. You have no choice in the matter. All our futures depend on it. Go, put your clothes on. Look as beautiful as you can. Be charming. You must find a way to make Mr. Bingley propose, and save us all."

∞ ∞ ∞

No matter how worried she was feeling about papa, Elizabeth reminded herself, she had to set it aside. Her mother was right. This was no time for self-indulgence or self-pity. She needed to be strong and to hold up her head. As she entered Netherfield, she put her worries behind her and focused on the task at hand. Why should she be any different from the thousands of young women before her who had done everything they could to secure advantageous marriages? She would take a page from Charlotte Lucas' book. Charlotte had very cleverly manipulated Mr. Collins into proposing to her, flattering his injured pride after Elizabeth's rejection of his proposal. She knew that marrying him would mean that eventually, she would be mistress of Longbourn.

She would not allow a vague desire to fall in love ruin her life. She was an intelligent young lady, after all. It was time to put aside childish daydreams. With a sense of regret, she let those daydreams go. It would have been nice, she mused, to find a meeting of true minds and hearts, but outside of Shakespeare's sonnets, real life beckoned. Romance was for school girls who had nothing better to do than to imagine a hero who would sweep them off their feet. Such gentlemen did not exist.

At least she had managed to counter mama's plans to compromise Mr. Bingley and force him into offering for her. She would never have forgiven herself if she had gone along with such a despicable strategy. How could she ever look Mr. Bingley in the face, knowing she had forced him into something he may not have wanted at all?

Taking a deep breath, and setting aside the turmoil inside her, she approached Mr. Bingley in the receiving line.

∞ ∞ ∞

As soon as Elizabeth joined the throng of guests, Maria Lucas came up to her.

"How is your father faring, Lizzy? Mama tells me he is very ill, and not likely to survive."

Elizabeth felt a jolt of shock at hearing it spoken of with so little sensitivity. Her soul recoiled from Maria's assessment of the situation. So Lady Lucas had heard already! News certainly travelled fast, considering that the rain had prevented her sisters from leaving the house.

"He is not precisely on his deathbed, Maria," she replied, severely. "We are hoping the fever will break soon."

"Of course you are," said Maria, with a pitying look. "But you have done the sensible thing to attend. You have to do everything you can to fix Mr. Bingley's attachment. Mama says there are several ladies vying for his affections, and if you don't catch him soon, you will lose him. Hopefully, you will drive them all away tonight. You must be careful not to smell of desperation, however. He must not know about the extent of your father's condition."

Elizabeth stared at Maria. Since when had her friend become so calculating? She used to be a very sweet girl. It was her mother's influence, no doubt. Very probably she was just repeating everything her mother had said.

"I will not smell of desperation, Maria, because I am not desperate. I wish you would not talk in this manner."

Maria shrugged. "I know it is difficult to accept, but you must. You cannot continue to live with your head in the clouds, Lizzy."

Elizabeth was becoming so incensed at Maria that she was about to say something unwise when Mr. Bingley approached to claim the first dance. Elizabeth had never been so relieved to end a conversation, and her smile of gratitude at Mr. Bingley for saving her from quarrelling with her closest friend was entirely free from artifice.

∞ ∞ ∞

Mr. Darcy's gaze was drawn repeatedly towards Miss Bennet as she danced and spoke with Bingley. What could Miss Bennet have to say to him? What was Bingley saying that amused Miss Bennet so much? For the first time since he had met her, Miss Bennet's conduct struck him as artificial. She was laughing too loudly and leaning in too much towards Bingley when he was talking to her. Darcy wanted to walk over and put a stop to it.

Miss Bingley, who had come to stand next to him, followed the direction of his gaze.

"I see what you are thinking, Mr. Darcy. Miss Bennet is flirting outrageously with Charles. Her conduct is quite disgraceful. She is no better than those sisters of hers."

Darcy, who was thinking exactly the same thing, immediately felt compelled to come to her defense. "Miss Bennet is completely different from her sisters. *They* cannot distinguish between one gentleman and another. Miss Bennet has shown no such tendency."

"That is not necessarily a virtue. It is because she is single-minded in her pursuit of my brother."

Darcy felt a sudden spike of anger against Miss Bingley. "Miss Bennet is not pursuing your brother. I rather think it is the other way. I wish you would not always blame everyone else for your brother's impulsive nature. You know as well as I that Bingley has a tendency to fall in and out of love at the drop of a hat."

Miss Bingley smiled. "I see you are determined to defend Miss Bennet, but you cannot defend her mother. Surely you can see that Mrs. Bennet is a fortune hunter of the worst kind. Or do you think her innocent as well?"

Darcy shook his head. "She is far from innocent, but she is not different from all the other mothers in the room. They are all throwing their daughters at your brother in the most obvious fashion. It's a wonder Mr. Bingley does not march out of the room in disgust."

That seemed to satisfy Miss Bingley, who gave a little laugh and, after standing next to Darcy for a few minutes, no doubt hoping he would ask her to dance, she moved away.

Darcy continued to watch Bingley as he danced with Elizabeth. She was a very graceful dancer. Even though there was something strained about her actions tonight, she still moved in a manner that was unpretentious. The light of the candles caught in her dark eyes and made them luminous.

He tried to determine how Bingley felt about her. Did he really care for her? He certainly seemed to pay her his undivided attention. However, Darcy could see no difference between the way he interacted with Miss Bennet and other infatuations Bingley had been caught up in. However, it was clear to anyone watching that they were in perfect accord.

A few minutes later, he no longer wanted to watch. It made him profoundly uncomfortable to do it, though he could not put his finger on it. He would have to put a word in Bingley's ear. His friend was dallying too openly with Miss Bennet. It would not do. The countryside was vastly different from the city, where practiced flirtations were the norm. In fact, he was in half a mind to go over and interrupt them at that very moment.

Luckily, the dance ended very soon afterwards, and Bingley went off to find his next partner. As the music started up again, Darcy realized that she was without a partner.

Perhaps this was the perfect moment to ask Miss Bennet for the first dance.

∞ ∞ ∞

"What does Mr. Darcy mean by staring at me in that manner?" Elizabeth asked Maria. He made her feel self-conscious, and she had to resist the instinct to look in the mirror and make sure there was nothing wrong with her appearance.

Maria shrugged. "I have no idea. He has to look at someone, I suppose. He is like a character from a Gothic novel." Maria shivered a little. "He stands in the shadows and watches."

Elizabeth gave her friend's arm a poke. "Now you are really allowing your imagination to run wild. Mr. Darcy may be a little morose, granted, but he is hardly the type to make a villain."

"Oh, no, look, he is coming this way! Do you think he overheard me? Perhaps he is coming here to confront me for what I said."

"Nonsense, Maria." It did seem odd, however, to choose the very moment when they were speaking of him to come in their direction.

"Miss Bennet, I wonder if you will do me the honor of dancing the coming set, if you do not have anyone written down."

"Allow me to consult my card, Mr. Darcy." She looked the dance card over, though she knew perfectly well that she had not promised the dance to anyone else. She did not want to make it easy for him.

"Mr. Darcy, I see that the next set is indeed free."

"Good, then I will return for you." With that he bowed, clicked his heels together and strode away.

"What a puzzle he is! If he wished to dance with you, Lizzy, why did he come all the way across the room to ask you, then not exchange a single word? He could have waited until the music had finished."

Elizabeth bit her lower lip and looked amused. "Perhaps he did hear you after all."

"No! Please say it is not so, Lizzy!"

"Of course not, Maria. I am only teasing. If that was his reason for interrupting our conversation, then he would have said something in his own defense."

Maria looked relieved. "True." The two ladies fell silent for a moment, considering the encounter. "I confess I find Mr. Darcy quite a mystery."

"He is a mystery I will solve, one of these days."

"Be careful not to tread on anyone's toes."

"I am too good of a dancer to tread on anyone's toes."

"I didn't mean it that way—" Maria protested in confusion.

Elizabeth's lips curled upwards. "I know you didn't. Maria, you must know by now that I love to tease. How long have you been my friend?"

"I suppose since Charlotte got married to Mr. Collins."

"More or less. Since our return from Hunsford. Remember Lady Catherine? Detestable woman!"

"You must not say such things, Lizzy. Sometimes I think you are determined to shock everyone."

"She *is* a detestable woman, Maria. Admit it. She is not above reproach just because she lives in a grand house and is your brother-in-law's patroness."

Maria giggled. "She is rather unlikeable, isn't she, even if she is a grand lady?"

"She is a grand bully, not a grand lady. Still, Mr. Collins thinks the world of her, and Charlotte knows how to deal with her, and she is generous in her attentions, I suppose, which is all that matters."

They discussed their time at Hunsford for several minutes longer, until Mr. Darcy came to claim Elizabeth for the set.

∞ ∞ ∞

Darcy had never liked dancing, but with Miss Bennet it did not feel like dancing at all. It was because her conversation was so stimulating, he forgot to pay attention to the steps. They came naturally. Besides, it was a pleasure to dance with someone who was so light on her feet, and who did not depend on him to guide her through the crush of people.

"You dance elegantly, Mr. Darcy. I see you have been taught by a good master."

If he had been Mr. Darcy of Pemberley, he would have suspected her of flattery, but since he was not, at least, not here and now, he took her statement as genuine. It surprised him.

"I have never been complimented on my dancing by a young lady, Miss Bennet. I do not believe my dancing is anything out of the ordinary. But you are correct in one thing. I did have a good dancing master. Meanwhile, may I return your compliment? I would like to say the same thing about your dancing master."

Her eyes twinkled. "Now I know you do not mean your compliment at all, Mr. Darcy."

"Whatever can you mean, Miss Bennet? I am always genuine in my compliments. I fail to see the point of praising someone without sincerity."

"Then you should meet my cousin Mr. Collins. He has a wealth of compliments at his disposal and he dispenses them liberally."

He smiled. "I take it you do not approve of your cousin?"

"Not at all. He does not even pretend to be genuine. He boasts of them as being carefully studied."

Darcy could not help chuckling at the chagrin on her face. "He must be a person of weak understanding."

"I am glad you think that, Mr. Darcy. Mama wanted me to marry him, and when he proposed, she was furious at me for refusing him. But I could not have endured either him or his patroness, Lady Catherine."

Darcy started at the name and missed a step. However, recovering quickly, he sought to divert the conversation to something safer.

"I dislike pretense of any kind," he declared.

No sooner had the words left his lips than he wondered at his hypocrisy. Not only did he sound like a pompous idiot, but he had no grounds to stand on. His whole identity was a sham. Miss Bennet did not even know his proper name. She believed him to be John Darcy. Well, it was not exactly a lie, but John was not a name Darcy had ever used.

"So do I, Mr. Darcy. Which brings me back to my original point. Practically everyone in Meryton has had the same dancing master. His lessons were dreadfully dreary, but he did teach us what we needed, I suppose. With four girls in the house who like to dance – I'm excluding my sister Mary, who doesn't, but who is always happy to play for us – we've had plenty of opportunities to practice."

"Well then, I will not compliment your dancing master. I will compliment you on your dancing instead, since it is clear you have become a good dancer entirely through your own effort."

"Since you assure me that your compliments are entirely sincere, I will respond by saying I am flattered that you think so."

They were driven away from each other by the steps. As they merged together again, she gave an arch smile. "We have done very well, so far, sir. We have managed to keep up a conversation for almost a quarter of the set."

She was aware of his weakness, then, and was referring to it indirectly. What a sly minx she was! He could not let her remark go unanswered. "Why do I have the feeling you are not speaking of yourself, Miss Bennet? I do not think you usually have any difficulty in maintaining a conversation during a dance."

"True, but it depends on one's partner, does it not? I am certain you don't have any difficulty keeping a conversation with Miss Bingley during a dance, but that is because you have known each other for some time."

She had echoed his own feelings so well it was uncanny. "Very true. It is refreshing, however, to converse easily with a person one has met recently."

"Yes." Miss Bennet answered, but she seemed distracted. She was looking down the line to where Bingley was dancing with Miss Lucas. Was she thinking of Bingley? Was she thinking how easy conversation was with him? Bingley had always had a cheerful disposition, even when the boys at school had tried to put him down for not being their equal. He always forgiven their cruelty.

"Mr. Bingley is generally liked wherever he goes," he remarked, and was surprised to find himself resenting it.

She did not try to pretend she was not thinking of his friend. At least she was honest. "He is certainly very well liked in this district."

Darcy wondered cynically how much of that was due to his fortune. He did not know why he was feeling embittered. Perhaps because he was looking at the world from the other side. He was not penniless by any means, but since he could not advertise his wealth, he may as well have been. Darcy wondered how Miss Bennet would have behaved towards him if she knew how large an estate he owned. Would she have been any different? Would she have been looking across the room at him instead?

In an attempt to distract her from Bingley, he went back to their previous conversation, hoping the subject of his aunt would not come up again.

"So, is Mr. Collins married now?" He said lightly. "Did his compliments hit their mark?"

"Yes," she said. "He is married to Sir William's daughter Charlotte."

All Miss Bennet's usual vivacity had disappeared. Her face had closed up. He had asked the wrong question. He wondered why the topic was so sensitive to her.

He decided to switch the conversation to something impersonal. "Have you read the book I lent you yet?" There could be no problem with that question.

Her expression became even more withdrawn. "I have not had a chance. I have been – occupied." Her face suddenly looked white, her dark eyes standing out in contrast. There were dark circles under her eyes, he noticed.

Darcy felt a rush of concern. She had been ill not too long ago. Perhaps all this dancing was not good for her. "You look as if you are about to faint, Miss Bennet."

"I never faint."

She had said the same at Netherfield just before she was ill. She had declared that she never fell ill.

"Nevertheless, I think it might be better if you sat out the rest of the dance."

To his surprise, she did not argue. She suddenly seemed drained of all energy. She allowed him to lead her off the dance floor to a seat near the window, completely indifferent to the curious glances being sent her way.

"Do you think you are going to swoon? Should I fetch your mother?"

"No!" The strength of her exclamation startled him. "Please do not tell her anything. I will just rest a little."

She was distraught. There was something very wrong here. She did not seem like someone ill. Had the conversation about Mr. Collins distressed her in some way?

Darcy pulled up a chair and sat opposite her. "Is there something amiss, Miss Bennet? I know you do not know me well, but if I can help in any way..."

She nodded. "I am sorry to spoil your evening, Mr. Darcy. I thought I would be able to do it, but I cannot." She was staring at her hands, avoiding his gaze.

"Do what?" he probed, gently.

She looked up. He was shocked at the change that had happened. One moment she was a cheerful young woman without a care in the world, the next she was on the verge of tears. Her lips were trembling.

"My father is very ill, Mr. Darcy. He is on his deathbed. I am beside myself with anxiety. I should never have attended this ball, but I listened to mama, who did not believe I could do anything to help him. But I cannot bear to be away, when something might happen—"

Darcy hesitated, aware of watching eyes, then reached out and gave her right hand a very quick squeeze. "I am very sorry to hear it, Miss Bennet. It is only natural to feel like this under the circumstances."

Darcy saw the situation all too clearly. Mrs. Bennet was behind this. She had forced her daughter to attend because she wanted her to capture Bingley. He pursed his lips to stop himself from saying something that would insult the mother and kept his attention on Elizabeth instead. Her head was bowed, and she was twisting her hands together.

"Would you prefer to return home? I will send for my carriage."

She looked up, her face brightening. "Would you, please? I think it is for the best. I can't—" She gestured towards the dancers.

"Of course. Stay here."

"Mr. Darcy," she said.

He turned back.

"Please do not inform my mother." Her face flushed with embarrassment.

Of course not. He nodded. "I won't. May I fetch your sister Mary to accompany you? I believe you said she doesn't care for dancing."

"Yes, that would be perfect."

Darcy made his way across the ballroom, ordered the carriage, then went to Bingley.

"Miss Bennet has to return home. Her father has taken ill and she wishes to attend to him."

Bingley's cheerful disposition clouded, and he looked glum. "Oh. I was so looking forward to sitting next to her at dinner!" He groaned. "Nothing to be done. Well, then, I had better take her home." He began to move, then stopped. "But how am I to do that? I cannot leave my guests."

"I will see to it that she gets home safely," said Darcy.

"Will you, Darcy?" Bingley clapped him on the shoulder. "You are a capital fellow. I know this will be uncomfortable for you, since you don't like conversing with strangers, but I am glad to hear she will be in safe hands. I will go to speak with her."

"Better not. She does not want to draw attention to her leaving and create speculation. We will go quietly."

"Quite right. Well then, I will leave it to you to handle it."

∞ ∞ ∞

The drive to Longbourn was silent. Darcy longed to comfort Elizabeth by taking her two hands or putting his arm around her. She would lean her head against his shoulder, and she would feel better. He knew what grieving felt like. It hurt him to know that he could do nothing to make matters easier.

With her sister Mary looking on, he couldn't even say anything. He was not sure whether Mary was aware of the severity of Mr. Bennet's condition. She had not objected when he had told her they were leaving, but she did not seem unduly upset.

As they approached Longbourn, it seemed cast in darkness. A candle flickered in the attic, where the servants were, and another one in an upstairs window.

"Is that your father's bedchamber?" he asked.

Elizabeth nodded.

He felt her dread as she fretted over whether Mr. Bennet had worsened during her absence.

"Shall I come in with you?" He asked, moments later, when the carriage came to a halt.

"Thank you, Mr. Darcy. I prefer to go up alone." Mary stepped out and Elizabeth followed quickly, then turned back and gave him her hand.

He took it briefly. Her fingers were cold even in her gloves.

"Can you have someone come down and tell me how he is?"

She nodded, then half-ran to the open door and disappeared outside. A short time later, he saw her shadow across the ceiling of the bedchamber.

He waited for some time, but nobody came. He sat there, considering, wondering why he cared so much what was happening to her. He could still feel the imprint of her hand in his palm. He had no idea how long he waited, but gradually, he realized that she had forgotten about him completely. He did not blame her, under the circumstances, but in the dark confines of the carriage, he felt more alone than he had ever been.

Eventually, he asked the coachman to drive him back to Netherfield. It was no use waiting for a message that would never come.

Chapter 11

*D*arcy woke up to an unpleasant feeling. The sensation was similar to having a nightmare, but he did not recall what he had dreamt, only the unpleasant aftermath. He lay in bed, trying to remember why he had such a twisted, knotted feeling in the pit of his stomach.

As he came out of sleep fully, he realized the sick feeling was not caused by a nightmare, but by the events of the night before. Apart from the feeling of happiness he had experienced while dancing with Miss Bennet, the rest of the evening had been nothing short of dismal.

It had all started when Darcy had returned to Netherfield, hoping to sneak upstairs and avoid the rest of the ball. However, Bingley had appeared in the hallway to waylay him as he started to ascend the stairs.

"I suspected you would go upstairs," said Bingley, snappishly. "I decided to come out as soon as I heard the carriage."

Darcy was taken aback by Bingley's tone. "I'm surprised you heard me above the noise of the ballroom."

"I was listening for you to return. In fact, I had dinner held back to wait for you. What the devil took you so long?"

There was a note of accusation to Bingley's question. Darcy had never been addressed like this by his long-term friend.

"What exactly are you implying, Bingley?"

"I'm not implying anything," Bingley replied, curtly, "only it took an inordinately long time for you to come back. It is only three miles to Longbourn."

"A six-mile journey back and forth, on a moonless night. I ask you again, what are you implying? Are you by any chance questioning my honor?" Darcy's voice was like steel.

Bingley blanched.

"Heavens, no, Darcy. I would never—"

"—or are you questioning Miss Bennet's honor? You are fully aware that her sister Mary, who is a very upright young lady, was with us in the carriage?"

Bingley looked shamefaced. "No, of course I'm not questioning – I don't know – it's just that you went away suddenly after you were dancing with her–" Bingley squeezed the bridge of his nose. "Confound it, Darcy. If you must have it, I was jealous. I wish I had been able to return her home."

He looked once again like an over-eager puppy, but Darcy had no patience for him, not tonight. "I am disappointed that you would even entertain such a thought, Mr. Bingley," he said in an icy tone, keeping his anger under strict control. "Miss Bennet was anxious about her father. She could not travel unaccompanied at night. I accompanied her, along with her sister."

Bingley shuffled his feet. "I know. Of course." His tone was apologetic. "It's just that I was so frustrated about Miss Bennet leaving, and you got to spend time with her."

He sounded sullen, almost childish.

Darcy's anger disappeared. He was overreacting. Of course Bingley was not implying anything disreputable. "Then let us say nothing further on the subject. I bid you goodnight."

"No!"

Darcy turned towards Bingley and raised his brow in question. Did Bingley intend to harp on the same subject again?

"I mean, you must come to supper. I had it especially held back for you."

If only Darcy had been decisive enough to continue on his way upstairs at that moment. However, it had been cold in the carriage, and Bingley's implied accusations had shaken him. Moreover, the old wound on his shoulder was aching, and his arm was growing stiff. He had hoped something warm to eat would take the chill from his bones and the presence of company would erase the bitter taste Bingley's questions had left.

"Very well. I will stay for supper, but I will leave as soon as it's over."

Bingley smiled, the normal hue returning to his face. "Good. I knew you would not take offence so easily. Come. Let us be friends. You know I would never doubt you."

Somehow, Darcy did not find those words particularly reassuring.

∞ ∞ ∞

The supper was much worse than even Darcy, in his most cynical mode, could have imagined, but ultimately, he did not regret attending, since it brought to the fore the issues that had been nagging him since the day Miss Bennet had come to stay in Netherfield.

It began with Sir William approaching him as everyone congregated to form the line of precedence to go in to supper.

"Mr. Darcy! Delighted to see you dance with Miss Bennet. You and Miss Bennet danced with such an elegant air." He leaned forward in a conspiring manner. "When a certain desirable event takes place, I hope to see you dance often, and with many a young lady. I am sure Mr. Bingley will be holding many such evenings in the future."

Darcy was stunned by Sir William's words. 'A certain desirable event?' Whatever did he mean? He was about to ask him, when Sir William clapped him on the shoulder and moved rapidly ahead to the front of the queue, leaving Darcy without the satisfaction of an answer.

If it had all ended there, Darcy would very likely have dismissed Sir William's statement. However, as it happened, he was seated opposite Mrs. Bennet and Lady Lucas. At first, he did not pay them much attention, since good manners dictated talking to his immediate neighbors, but it soon became impossible not to hear what Mrs. Bennet was saying since she was speaking freely and openly to Lady Lucas in a loud voice.

It was immediately apparent that the topic of the conversation was the expectation that Lizzy would be soon married to Mr. Bingley. It was an animating subject, and Mrs. Bennet seemed incapable of fatigue while enumerating the advantages of the match. His being such a charming young man, and so rich, and living but three miles from them, were the first points of self-gratulation; and then it was such a comfort to think how fond the two sisters were of dear Lizzy, and to be certain that they must desire the connection as much as she could do. It was, moreover, such a promising thing for her younger daughters, as Lizzy's marrying so well must throw them in the way of other rich men; and lastly, it was so pleasant at her time of life to be able to consign her single daughters to the care of their sister, that she might not be obliged to go into company more than she liked.

Darcy's attention was entirely fixed by Mrs. Bennet's conversation. At first, he listened with indignant contempt, but the horror of her words soon began to sink in. She was utterly shameless, to be boasting so openly of Miss Bennet's conquest of Bingley, but the reaction of Lady Lucas showed that no one was surprised by this possibility. Lady Lucas was listening with half-bored indifference, and at no instance did she raise any objections or try to moderate Mrs. Bennet's enthusiasm by pointing out that Bingley had not yet made an offer. It seemed everyone took it for granted. The significance of Sir William's words now struck him forcibly. So that was the 'happy event' to which he had referred!

At first Darcy was indignant because of his friend, who was unaware of all the expectations his partiality for Miss Bennet had awakened. Then, as he listened further, a leaden feeling coursed through his limbs. What if Bingley actually decided to ask Miss Bennet to marry him? It was clear from the way she had behaved with Bingley tonight that she was encouraging him, and equally clear what her answer would be.

Mrs. Bennet's open recitation of the advantages of the match further infuriated him. She made no attempt whatsoever to disguise her mercenary motives. Seeing them outlined in that cold-blooded manner sickened Darcy. He grew so agitated he had the appalling image of himself standing up, throwing down his napkin, and telling Mrs. Bennet that she was delusional, that Bingley would never marry her daughter. He was able with great difficulty to stifle that impulse, and to somehow remain seated. However, his appetite was completely destroyed, and he sat rigidly on his chair in complete silence, too distressed to do anything except wait for the interminable meal to end.

∞ ∞ ∞

As the last of the carriages moved down the driveway – among them Mrs. Bennet's, whose apologies for Elizabeth's sudden departure conveniently delayed her departure – Bingley turned to Darcy and his sisters. Darcy had maintained his silence during supper and had withdrawn for some time when the dancing resumed. However, he was too gripped by anxiety to stay in his bedchamber for the night, and the compulsion to address the issue of Miss Bennet was too strong. As the ball drew to a close, he joined Bingley in bidding farewell to the guests, hoping for an opportunity to speak to Bingley about Mrs. Bennet's claims.

As the door closed, Bingley looked around. "Well, what do you think? Do you think it went well?"

"Yes," said Miss Bingley. "I would say it was a success. I am sure it was better than anything they have ever had here in Meryton."

Bingley, however, seemed preoccupied, and his expression was glum.

"If only Miss Bennet had not left so early."

This was the opening Darcy had been waiting for. He seized it immediately.

"It was just as well that Miss Bennet had to leave," said Darcy. "You have been paying her too much attention. There is a great deal of speculation about your relationship with her. There is even talk of marriage." He tried to say it casually, though he practically choked on the words. "Perhaps it would be best if you were to pay her less attention. You do not want her reputation to be affected when you leave."

Bingley looked astounded.

"When I leave? But I have no intention of leaving! Netherfield is my home now."

"Charles," said Miss Bingley, touching her brother on the shoulder. "You know very well that in a matter of weeks you will be tired of Meryton and longing to return to London."

Bingley shrugged off her hand. "But I love it here. I feel completely at home. I don't see why you would think that I would prefer to return to London."

"Because," said Miss Bingley, "you always grow restless when we go to a house party or a visit to friends, and quickly crave the excitement of London."

"This is different. I am not a guest. This is my own residence. This is what you have always wanted for me, Caroline. If you are growing tired of Netherfield, you are welcome to leave. Do not feel obliged to stay on just because I am."

"It is not a matter of staying or leaving, Charles," said Mrs. Hurst. "It is knowing what is expected of you. Mr. Darcy was pointing out that if you continue to show such a preference for Miss Bennet, people will expect you to marry her."

Bingley looked from one to the other.

"You are the ones making assumptions. I am certain no one else has noticed."

"Ah, but there you are wrong, Bingley. I was seated opposite Mrs. Bennet, and I can testify that she spent most of supper planning for your future with her daughter."

Bingley looked struck by that information. Good, thought Darcy, now that he is cornered, he will surely comprehend his folly.

"Did she really? That is the best news I have heard! It means there can be no objection to my being in trade. Mr. Bennet is a gentleman, you know, and I made certain to let him know that my father made his money from mining. I was afraid he would turn Miss

Bennet against me." Bingley paused. "When you took Miss Bennet home, I thought – never mind what I thought, but I believed her family was opposed to the match." He beamed. "You know what that means. It means I can offer for her."

Miss Bingley gave a cry. "Charles! You cannot!"

Mrs. Hurst shouted for her husband. "Mr. Hurst, you must come at once. Charles has lost his mind."

"You cannot offer for Miss Bennet," said Darcy, seized by a strong agitation. "You have only met with her a few times. You cannot know your own mind yet."

"Of course I know my own mind," said Bingley, unperturbed. "I know she is an angel, and I am in love with her. Her family has no objection, and I do believe Miss Bennet is partial to me. Frankly, I am at a loss to understand your reactions."

Darcy wished he could take hold of Bingley and shake some sense into him. How could he be so unreasonable? How could he be so blind to his own nature? Did he not remember how many times he had thought himself violently in love only to discover his ardor had cooled within a week?

It had been a terrible mistake for Bingley to take an estate in Netherfield. It was his first experience as a landowner, and he was unaccustomed to being admired and bowed to by all and sundry. It had gone to his head. And to think Miss Bennet would make him a good wife! Didn't he see he was throwing away everything his father had worked so hard for? Just when the Bingleys were on the verge of being accepted by Society, now, in one fell swoop, Bingley was willing to throw it all away for a passion that would not last a fortnight.

"But Charles, of course they wouldn't care you are in trade. Mr. Bennet may be a gentleman, but he married poorly. Mrs. Bennet is certainly not a gentleman's daughter. The whole family is ill-bred.

Look at her sisters! They flirt with every man that comes within a mile of them."

"I don't care about her family, Caroline. They seem perfectly respectable to me. I don't know why you constantly malign them."

"What? You don't think having an uncle who lives in *Cheapside* a problem?"

"She can have all the uncles in the world in Cheapside, what does it matter? She is a charming young lady."

"*You* may have no objections, Bingley," said Darcy, "but the fact is, it diminishes Miss Bennet's chances of having a good marriage. With a family like that, no gentleman of any consequence will have her." The words held the clear, cold weight of logic. There was no escaping that reality. Darcy thought then of the way Mrs. Bennet had bragged about having caught Bingley. "Besides, Mrs. Bennet is utterly vulgar and can only diminish your social consequence."

Bingley shook his head. "I know it is a shock to all of you, but I assure you I know what I'm doing. It is my decision, after all. Now, if you will excuse me, it has been a long evening and I need to retire. We will discuss this tomorrow, if you wish, but I can assure you, my mind is quite made up."

And with that, he ran up the stairs, taking it two steps at a time, and whistling a tune that the musicians had played when Bingley was dancing with Miss Bennet.

Chapter 12

Mr. Bennet's health continued to worsen, and Elizabeth was beside herself with worry. She wished desperately there was something she could do. The helplessness of her position was very apparent. Apart from dribbling a few spoonfuls of broth into his parched mouth or squeezing out wet clothes for his forehead to reduce the fever, there was little she could do to assist him. She worried that any moment now his condition would worsen dramatically. She did not dare leave his side.

The next day continued much the same. Elizabeth could think of nothing else. Every move Mr. Bennet made was anxiously observed. At moments, when he was quiet, Elizabeth's thoughts drifted to Mr. Bingley, wondering why he had not called to ask after her father, and to Mr. Darcy, whose quiet presence had given her strength just when she had needed it.

Thursday saw the arrival of a London physician sent from Netherfield. Elizabeth was relieved on two counts. The first was the possibility that the physician might do something for papa. The second was the knowledge that Mr. Bingley had thought of her after all. She felt a rush of gratitude to him for his solicitous kindness.

Mr. Lockridge was a tall, gaunt man who said very little. However, Elizabeth was reassured by his manner of quiet efficiency. After examining Mr. Bennet at length, he took Elizabeth aside.

"There is hope," said Mr. Lockridge. "If he has not succumbed with such a high fever, then it means his body is still fighting. He is too ill for extensive bloodletting, but I know of a physician who travelled to the far east who advocates drawing a small amount of blood to drain the fever. I have seen it work on numerous occasions."

"If you think it will help," said Elizabeth, "then by all means try it."

"I may require your assistance. You will need to hold him. He may toss and turn when I cut him."

"Of course."

∞ ∞ ∞

After Elizabeth saw Mr. Lockridge out, Mrs. Bennet came rushing out of the parlor to intercept Elizabeth.

"I would have gone in, but I heard the physician speak about bloodletting. I cannot abide the sight of blood. I was sure I would faint. Is Mr. Bennet any better?"

"It's too early to tell if Mr. Lockridge's treatment helped," said Elizabeth.

"How generous of Mr. Bingley to bring him from London! How considerate! I think we should invite him to dinner tomorrow, so we can have a chance to thank him."

"I do not think that would be appropriate, mama, when papa is so ill."

"Nonsense, child. We cannot all starve, just because your father is too ill to join us. Besides, you must make sure Mr. Bingley does not forget you." She paused, considering. "I suppose I shall have to invite his sisters, and that despicable Mr. Darcy, too. I saw you were obliged to stand up with him. Never mind. Mr. Bingley will be offering for you any day now. If only Mr. Bennet was well enough to shoot some pheasants. I don't know what to serve at this time of the year."

Elizabeth was horrified at the direction of her mother's thoughts.

"How can you even think of having a dinner party when papa might be—?"

She could bear it no longer. Rather than say something unpleasant, she left the room, with Mrs. Bennet calling after her that she was a silly child who did not know her own good.

Later that afternoon, when she came downstairs for some tea, a small parcel arrived for her from Netherfield. She unwrapped the brown paper to find a leather-bound copy of Coleridge's *Friends* with a brief note. The note said simply:

To read at Mr. Bennet's bedside. This might help you take your mind off things. D

Mrs. Bennet practically tore the note from Elizabeth's fingers then tossed it aside after she had read it.

"Oh, I hoped it might be from Mr. Bingley, but 'tis only from that man. What do you need more books for? Have you told him that your father has a library already? He probably thinks we're too poor to own any books. He must have taken this one from Mr. Bingley's library."

Elizabeth knew Mr. Darcy must have ordered a copy especially from London, because Mr. Clarke only owned one copy, the one she had been reading when she had first met Mr. Darcy, and that copy had not been so well bound. She also knew that Mr. Bingley did not care much for reading, so would be unlikely to own the book. She was growing tired of her mother's constant criticism of Mr. Darcy.

"He meant it kindly, mama," she said.

"Well, send it back. Tell him you have plenty of books of your own to read."

"I will not. I don't wish to cause offence."

"Why should we care about giving offence to a penniless nobody?"

"We don't know that Mr. Darcy is penniless, mama."

Mrs. Bennet sniffed. "If he were rich, why would he conceal it from everyone? There's something not quite right about Mr. Darcy, I'm telling you. You had better keep your distance, Lizzy."

"I am keeping my distance. He was thoughtful enough to send a book to keep me occupied while I keep vigil at my father's bedside, that is all."

Mrs. Bennet sniffed and said nothing else, only it was quite clear she did not approve.

The fact was that Elizabeth had been touched by the gesture. Mr. Darcy had been so good to her the night of the Netherfield ball, and now he was trying what he could to lift her spirits. Her thoughts went back to the time she had spent with him at the ball. Dancing with him had briefly banished her worry about her father. She had enjoyed pitting her wits against him, and then, afterwards, he had been very sympathetic when she was upset. It had been inconvenient for him to be forced to leave the ball to accompany her to Longbourn, but he had known exactly what she needed. He had not tried to distract her with empty conversation, yet his presence in the carriage had been reassuring.

They had connected on previous occasions as well. When they had first met at Clarke's, he had not taken offence at her teasing manner. Then, during dinner at Sir Williams', he had known that she was trying to solicit information from him and had cleverly side-stepped her questions. Her recollection of those occasions made her smile. He was arrogant, true, but she felt that in some ways he understood her.

Nevertheless, she reminded herself sharply, she did not trust Mr. Darcy. There was an aloofness about him that she didn't like, and she was certain he was concealing something unsavory about his past. She knew absolutely nothing about him. She was simply making too much of the fact that he had been compassionate when she was in a difficult situation.

Still, she thought, as she settled once again in the armchair at the foot of Mr. Bennet's bed, there was something very comforting about the feel of a leather volume in her hands.

∞ ∞ ∞

Three days after the Netherfield ball, Darcy stood at the window of the library and watched Bingley riding away. Exhausted and drained after a very unpleasant morning, Darcy tried to quash the niggling feeling of guilt that was surfacing at the view of Bingley's hunched shoulders. Darcy did not doubt he had done the right thing, nor did he regret it, but he did not enjoy the knowledge that he was instrumental in making his friend very unhappy.

Well, it was done. He and Bingley's sisters had joined forces and used all their persuasive powers to convince Bingley that he needed to wait before committing to a serious undertaking like marriage. It had taken three days. Bingley had been unusually stubborn. He had insisted that he was going to marry Miss Bennet, whatever happened. Even when he'd finally agreed to give himself some time away from Miss Bennet, just to be absolutely certain, Bingley had sworn he would be back.

The sick feeling that Darcy had experienced when he had awakened three days ago was still there, but it had become more of a gnawing ache. As Bingley disappeared around the corner, Darcy moved away from the window and settled into the armchair with a book, but found it impossible to focus on the words.

After several minutes of trying, he gave up and went to the desk instead. He had started a letter to Georgiana two days ago and he needed to finish it. At least he could do something useful.

Dear Sister,

I did not expect to be writing to you again so soon, but I have taken refuge in the library once again because a crisis has arisen. We are in such an uproar here.

You know I wrote to you about Miss Bennet? Well, Bingley has declared his intention to marry her. Caroline is in a fit of hysterics. Even Mr. Hurst, who can seldom rouse himself long enough to take any interest in anything but food, is horrified at Bingley's folly. For folly it surely is. I have nothing against Miss Bennet herself. She is a very agreeable young lady, but if you had been at the ball you would have witnessed the lack of breeding displayed by the rest of the family, in particular the younger daughters. The worst culprit is the abominable Mrs. Bennet, who has been boasting to all and sundry that poor Bingley is going to propose to Miss Bennet any moment! Shameless woman! I am completely out of patience with her scheming manner.

Meanwhile, Bingley has decided Miss Bennet is the only woman he will ever marry. We have tried to remind him that this is not the first time he had fallen in love, and very probably not the last, but to no avail. It is really most unfortunate. Bingley is impulsive, granted, but he has never done anything really reckless before. He is throwing away his happiness as well as that of his sister over a momentary infatuation.

I have spoken to Miss Bingley and we are both agreed that the best course of action would be to remove Bingley from Netherfield immediately. However, short of forcing him to drink laudanum and bundling him by force into a carriage, I am not yet certain how to convince him. Here is Miss Bingley now—I need to discuss the matter with her. I will write more later.

It is Friday and we have managed -- with great difficulty – to convince Bingley not to enter into any engagement until at least a month of reflection has passed. Bingley balked at the prospect of a separation, but I have persuaded him that a postponement of his happy state will have no negative effect on either of them. Hopefully the distractions of London will cure him of this ill-fated connection. He is now on the road to Town. I know we have made him very unhappy, but it is for his own good.

I must end this letter now if I am to get it out by the afternoon post. I hope all is well with you, Georgiana.

Your affectionate brother William

∞ ∞ ∞

On Friday morning, Elizabeth, who was dozing in the armchair in her father's bedchamber, woke up with a feeling that something had changed. Groggily, she tried to work out what it was. Then she realized that the restless tossing about of Mr. Bennet had ceased.

With a cry, she jumped to her feet, terrified of what she would discover. As she approached the bed, she saw that Mr. Bennet was lying completely still. A sob rose to her throat.

It was over.

She knelt at the side of the bed and took his hand between hers. She should go downstairs and tell mama, she knew, but she needed a moment alone with papa before everything descended into chaos.

"Lizzy, is that you?"

She started. There was no mistaking that voice. She looked towards her father and found his eyes open. He was looking at her with eyes clear of fever.

"Papa!" she said, throwing herself at him. "You are recovered! Thank heavens!"

She began to sob again, this time with joy and relief.

"Now, now," said Mr. Bennet. "No need to make such a fuss. How long have I been ill?"

"Almost a week."

"A week? That's a long time. I'm sorry I caused you such anxiety. If you don't mind, though, I think I'm going to sleep. I feel completely exhausted."

"I very much doubt you're going to get much sleep, especially when mama finds out you're out of danger."

"Well, you'd better go down and get it over with, then. I'll do my best to wait for your mother's effusions before I go to sleep, but I can't promise anything."

Elizabeth smiled with happiness, kissed him on the brow, and went downstairs to tell everyone the good news.

∞ ∞ ∞

Mrs. Bennet had yielded to Elizabeth's persuasions not to invite Bingley for dinner until Mr. Bennet's situation became clear. Elizabeth had managed to convince her that inviting Bingley while the master of the house was dangerously ill might be considered bad taste. However, now that Mr. Bennet had recovered, she didn't want to lose a second more. Accordingly, she sent a servant to Netherfield with a note to invite Bingley and his party for dinner the next day.

The afternoon brought a note from Netherfield. It was addressed to Elizabeth.

"Hurry, Lizzy, and tell me," said Mrs. Bennet. "Does he accept the invitation?"

Elizabeth opened the note. She could tell at once it wasn't from Mr. Bingley from the feminine writing and the scent of roses that emanated from the paper.

Dear Miss Bennet,

I am writing to let you know that Mr. Bingley has been called away unexpectedly to Town. We are not at all certain when he will be able to return, but I know he plans to spend Christmas with friends. I regret to say we will not be able to accept your mother's invitation for tomorrow due to another engagement.

Your dear friend, Caroline Bingley

Scarcely able to believe this unexpected turn of events, Elizabeth read the letter again, to make certain she hadn't missed anything.

She felt numb. No one had said anything about leaving for London at all, certainly not Mr. Bingley, who had talked as if he expected to experience the Christmas season in Meryton for the first time as a landlord. Something unexpected must have happened.

"Well?" prompted Mrs. Bennet.

Elizabeth looked up to see her mother and sisters watching her expectantly.

She shook her head. "Not good news, I'm afraid. It is from Miss Bingley. Mr. Bingley has been called away to London, and his sisters have a prior engagement."

"Did Miss Bingley say when he is coming back?"

"No, she gave no indication, but not before Christmas."

Mrs. Bennet grabbed the note from Elizabeth's hands and read through it.

"Well, I am sure Mr. Bingley will not stay away long." She considered the matter for a few moments, then her face brightened. "I think I know what Mr. Bingley is up to. He has gone to choose an engagement gift. He wants it to be a surprise."

Elizabeth stared at her mother and shook her head. She did not believe that for a moment.

Chapter 13

r. Bennet recovered faster than anyone expected, and within ten days no one could have guessed that the Bennet family had been on the brink of disaster. Mrs. Bennet made it known that her husband's recovery was due to Mr. Lockridge's fortunate intervention. Since Mr. Lockridge had been sent for by Mr. Bingley, the natural conclusion was that it was Mr. Bingley who had saved Mr. Bennet's life. Every possible positive attribute was given to Mr. Bingley. He was eagerly awaited, and every new morning brought fresh hope that today he would return with his surprise engagement gift.

A few days later, a letter arrived from Netherfield. Luckily, Mrs. Bennet and her daughters were not at home, and Elizabeth was able to open it privately. She started to read it eagerly, expecting news of Mr. Bingley's return, but it was from Miss Bingley. It was a long, rambling letter, but after reading it several times in disbelief, Elizabeth discovered that the whole family was moving to London, and that it was unlikely that they would come to Netherfield in the near future. It suggested that Mr. Bingley was leading an active life away from Meryton, was at a hunting party with friends in the north, and had all but forgotten her existence.

The letter was a blow. She had been hesitant at times about marrying Mr. Bingley and had declared herself willing to do it only if he sincerely cared for her. Now it appeared he did not, and she did not know how to deal with it. At times, Elizabeth thought herself resigned, but then one of the neighbors would ask about him and she would feel the chagrin and discomfort of not having answers. She felt ill-used, and wondered if he had ever cared about her at all.

Then at other times, she would remember something he said or an expression on his face, and she would be certain he cared for her, and that he would return.

Meanwhile, she had heard that Mr. Darcy was still residing in Netherfield. She expected to meet him in Meryton, and made sure to go to Clarke's Circulating Library every Tuesday, but she did not so much as catch a glimpse of him. Upon questioning Mr. Clarke, she was told that Mr. Darcy preferred to have his books sent directly to Netherfield rather than coming in.

She was at a loss how to account for these sudden changes. She wanted to talk to Mr. Darcy, to find out what had happened to make both gentlemen avoid her. Whatever the charges against her might be, she surely had the right to defend herself, after all.

When it was clear that she would not come upon Mr. Darcy by chance, she tried to convince Mrs. Bennet to invite him, arguing that he would be able to give them the latest news of Bingley, but Mrs. Bennet would not hear of it. Her dislike and prejudice against Mr. Darcy was too strong. Elizabeth soon heard from Maria that there would have been little point in inviting him anyway, since he rarely accepted any invitations. He had agreed to dine with Sir William on Christmas day, but other than that, he seemed determined to keep to himself.

Three weeks passed, and Christmas was upon them. On the twenty-third of December, Mrs. Bennet's brother Gardiner and his family came down from London for the celebrations. Mrs. Bennet by now had placed all her expectations in Miss Bingley's first letter. She held the firm belief that Miss Bingley had said that Mr. Bingley would return after Christmas, and she began to make preparations to receive him once Twelfth Night was over. Although Elizabeth had told her of the second letter, Mrs. Bennet had chosen to ignore it.

That evening, listening to Mrs. Bennet's praise of Mr. Bingley, Aunt Gardiner took Elizabeth aside and asked her about him.

"Is he as remarkable as your mother makes him sound, Lizzy?"

Elizabeth gave a rueful smile. "Mama presents him as nothing short of a god. He is a mere mortal, I'm afraid. However, he is both handsome and rich, which certainly goes a long way towards defining his character."

"Do you love him, then, Lizzy?"

"I believe I do, just a little. I am not passionately in love, but his unexpected departure has affected my spirits."

Mrs. Gardiner patted her kindly on the arm and expressed her wishes that he would soon rejoin them.

Elizabeth gnawed at her lip and said nothing. She was by no means confident that he would return. She had a strong feeling that Miss Bingley did not approve of her, and that she would do everything in her power to separate her brother from Elizabeth. Whether he would come back, decided Elizabeth, depended entirely on whether he was able to stand up to his sister.

It pained her to think that he could not.

∞　∞　∞

On Christmas day, the Gardiners and the Bennets attended church, as was customary. To her surprise, as Elizabeth entered the parish church, she spotted Mr. Darcy sitting at the back, his head bowed. Her immediate impulse was to go over to him at once, but since she could not do so without being noticed, she contented herself with standing in the isle and calling out to him.

"Mr. Darcy! I see you have decided to emerge from your shell."

He looked startled that she had addressed him, and a flush of color touched his cheeks.

The corners of his lips turned up in a small smile. "I suppose by that you mean to compare me to a turtle."

"No, because the destiny of turtles is to end up in turtle soup. I meant to compare you to a snail."

"Thank you," he said, with a small laugh. "I do not know whether that is a terrible insult or a compliment."

"Neither, it is simply a comment on your hermetic tendencies."

Mrs. Bennet tugged at Elizabeth's sleeve.

"Come along, Lizzy. You can't stand here blocking the aisle. Let's take our seats." She gave Mr. Darcy a cold curtsey. "Merry Christmas, Mr. Darcy."

Elizabeth wrinkled her nose comically and shrugged. He smiled as Mrs. Bennet pulled Elizabeth along with her.

The encounter lifted Elizabeth's spirits. The gloom that had settled over her lightened. She scarcely attended to anything the vicar said. She was conscious all through the service of Mr. Darcy sitting at the back and had to stop herself several times from looking in his direction.

∞ ∞ ∞

Darcy had hesitated about whether to attend church on Christmas day or not, but the habit of many years prevailed. He had expected to see Miss Bennet, of course, and had planned to give her a curt nod and move on, but when she had addressed him he had found himself swept up in the moment.

He was glad he had chosen to sit at the back. It gave him the opportunity to feast his eyes on those dark, shining locks without anyone noticing. As usual, she had made him laugh with her absurd comments. He had almost winked at her, but decided it was too intimate a gesture. There was something about Miss Bennet that made him behave uncharacteristically. She made him lose himself in the moment.

At first, the pleasure of knowing she was there under the same roof was enough, but the longer he sat, the more restless he became. He wanted more than anything to get up and sit beside her, or behind her, somewhere where he could be close and relish her presence. He forced himself to stay in place during the interminable sermon and was excessively relieved when they came to the last hymn. He thought he could distinguish her sweet voice among the singers. It was balm to his soul.

He was one of the last to leave, pretending to fumble with the prayer book as he waited for the Bennets to join the line of well-wishers to greet the vicar. He approached them as they stood around speaking to the rest of the congregation.

"Mr. Bennet," he said. "I had heard of your recovery. I hope you did not suffer any ill-effects from your illness."

"Very kind of you to enquire," said Mr. Bennet. "I have recovered fully, though I hope I will never have to experience such a fever again."

"I hope Mr. Lockridge proved to be a help. He has been the family physician for some years now, but he is always searching for new cures."

Mr. Bennet was looking at him closely and Darcy realized he had unwittingly revealed something of his background. He wanted to kick himself for such a silly mistake, but he could not think of a way to cover his tracks.

"Ah, so it was you who sent for Mr. Lockridge," said Elizabeth, brightly. "I had thought it was Mr. Bingley. Allow me, sir, to express my heartfelt thanks. I do not believe papa would have pulled through if it were not for him."

With several eyes upon him, Darcy felt profoundly uncomfortable.

As if sensing his discomfort, Mr. Bennet shifted the conversation to the subject of hunting.

"Mr. Gardiner and I are planning to go hunting on the next clear day. I hope you will join us, Mr. Darcy. The pheasants are growing fat and lazy and we would welcome an extra hand and some company."

Darcy would have declined, only Miss Bennet's fine eyes were upon him and he could not bring himself to say no.

"I would be honored, sir."

"Good," said Mr. Bennet. "I look forward to it."

Darcy was rewarded with a smile from Miss Bennet, and he departed with a light step and a cheerful heart. It had been a good decision to come to the service, after all.

∞ ∞ ∞

Thursday dawned bright and clear, and true to his word, Mr. Bennet sent word early, asking for Mr. Darcy to join him and his brother-in-law.

Darcy arrived promptly to find the two gentlemen waiting for him by the stables. He dismissed the tinge of disappointment he experienced at not being invited into the house. It was obviously too early for the ladies to be up and about. It was just that he enjoyed his encounters with Miss Bennet and had hoped to exchange a few words with her, however briefly.

He reminded himself, not for the first time, that it would not do. Miss Bennet was enchanting, admittedly, but he needed to take a leaf from Bingley's book and avoid her completely, before he, too, succumbed to her charms.

Mr. Gardiner, Darcy was pleased to discover, was a well-bred gentleman with a quick mind and a pleasant temperament. They were soon engaged in conversation, and the morning passed very agreeably. It was a crisp winter day, and it was stimulating to be in the great outdoors.

By and by, the conversation turned to the subject he was dreading: Netherfield, and Mr. Bingley's absence. He had hoped he would not have to answer questions about it, but of course it was impossible to avoid.

"Will Mr. Bingley be re-joining you soon at Netherfield?"

There is nothing in Mr. Bennet's tone that suggested anything more than plain curiosity, but Darcy cursed inwardly. How was he going to justify staying behind at Netherfield if Bingley was not planning to return? He searched quickly for a convincing answer.

"Mr. Bingley has business elsewhere. I have agreed to stay behind and oversee the estate."

Mr. Bennet looked surprised. "As a kind of steward?"

It galled Darcy that he had to play such a role. It went against every instinct, but he had no choice in the matter. It was only one more role he was obliged to play since the tragic event that had changed his life.

A partial truth would serve best here. "Only informally. Mr. Bingley is a friend, but he has no experience at all in managing an estate, and he has other matters to attend to. I have promised to help him out, unofficially."

At least he would not appear like a paid employee. He wondered if Mr. Bennet was the sort who would snub him because of his standing.

Mr. Bennet nodded. "Well, then, I expect we shall see a lot of each other if you are to stay at Netherfield for some time. Are you fond of eels, Mr. Darcy? If you are still here in February, we can go elver dipping. I have a good size pond, with plenty of eels."

Mr. Bennet's easy acceptance filled him with a strange feeling. It humbled him that Mr. Bennet welcomed him regardless of his social status. Darcy looked at Mr. Bennet with fresh eyes. He had misjudged him. He was a good, solid country gentleman. Perhaps, in time, he might even make a good friend. For the first time, Darcy felt there was an advantage to being unknown. It gave him a clearer idea of who his friends really were.

As they approached Longbourn, Mr. Bennet invited him for dinner that night, as was the custom, but Darcy politely refused, claiming he had matters to take care of at Netherfield. They parted at the gate and Darcy turned back towards Bingley's estate.

He would have loved to dine in Miss Bennet's presence, but he wanted to tread carefully. His rational mind warned him he should avoid Miss Bennet altogether. His conscience reminded him that Bingley wanted to marry her. He could not betray his friend, not until he was satisfied that it was only a temporary madness. His heart, however, clamored to go inside.

In the end, his conscience and his mind won. However, it was deuced hard to walk away knowing he could have spent the evening under the same roof as Miss Bennet.

Chapter 14

The Christmas festivities were over. Mr. and Mrs. Gardiner had returned to London with their children, and the house was now back to its usual self. The Gardiners were sorely missed by Elizabeth, who could not help brooding over the reasons for Mr. Bingley's abrupt disappearance. It did not help that Mrs. Bennet took every opportunity she could to tell Elizabeth she must have done or said something to drive Mr. Bingley away.

"We all know you tend to let your tongue run away with you. It is almost certain – nay, I am convinced – that you frightened him away with something you said."

"I did not, mama. I said nothing at all that could possibly cause him to be upset."

"Think back, Lizzy. There must be a reason, otherwise, why would he take up and leave so very suddenly?"

"Don't you think I have considered that, mama? I have thought back very carefully, but there is nothing at all that indicated to me that Mr. Bingley was planning to leave. On the contrary, he led me to believe that he would be calling on me in a private matter."

Elizabeth pressed the bridge of her nose. She could not help feeling that she must have done something wrong. Perhaps Mr. Bingley had been insulted that she had left the ball with Mr. Darcy. But if that was the case, surely he would have given her a chance to defend herself?

There was really no explanation. Everything was going just as it should be, then, puff! Mr. Bingley was gone.

His disappearance was as much of a mystery as Mr. Darcy's past continued to be. Was it possible the two things were related?

Fortunately for her spirits, an old friend of hers, Miss Ruth Clapp, came to visit Meryton from Southampton with her aunt a few days later and proved to be just the kind of distraction Elizabeth needed. They reminisced about their childhood, and Elizabeth brought Ruth up to date with the events that had led up to Bingley's departure.

Two days after Miss Clapp's arrival, on a sunny January morning, the two ladies called on Maria Lucas, and invited her to walk up with them to Oakham Mount, and soon the three friends were skipping across the open countryside, arms linked, laughing merrily and singing a silly little song.

Maria broke off suddenly in warning, indicating the outline of a horseman against the horizon. "We have company."

The three ladies stopped skipping at once and separated self-consciously, slowing to a proper walk. The rider was too far away to identify clearly, but Elizabeth recognized the arrogant upright posture of Mr. Darcy. She earnestly hoped he hadn't seen them. He would no doubt think her just as wild as her sisters. Well-bred young ladies did not skip around in public.

"I think it's Mr. Darcy," said Maria, shading her eyes and squinting.

"Good. I am eager to meet the mysterious Mr. Darcy," said Miss Clapp. "How fortunate that I will encounter him so soon after I arrived."

"Be warned," said Elizabeth, "He is such an odd mix of reticence and arrogance that no one can make head or tails of him."

"He sounds intriguing."

Elizabeth kept an eye on the figure on horseback, feeling a thrill of anticipation as she waited for him to draw closer. However, he turned at an angle and took off in a fast gallop in a different direction. Elizabeth was disappointed, but after a moment's consideration, she was glad he had not spotted them.

"So where were we before Mr. Darcy interrupted us?" She linked arms again with her two friends and they went back to skipping.

∞ ∞ ∞

It was an unseasonably warm day, and with nothing urgent awaiting him at Netherfield, Darcy was reluctant to hide himself indoors again. He took the ridgeway across to Oakham Mount, allowing the horse full rein, feeling the wind in his hair as they galloped across the open landscape. The chalk grassland was soft under the horse's feet and for the first time for months he felt the simple joy of being outdoors. They slowed down as the path to the Mount grew steeper, and Darcy dismounted to walk up the hill.

It was not long before he heard women's laughter, interspersed with singing. Darcy's heart leapt as he recognized the unmistakable husky voice of Miss Bennet. Her laugh set his pulse racing. He stood completely still, trying to compose himself, hoping they would not come across him when he was still flustered. They were just behind the small grassy mound that marked the top of the hill and would be upon him any moment.

As he gathered his chaotic thoughts into focus, it occurred to him that they would not be expecting anyone to be here. Not wanting to startle them, he cleared his throat loudly to warn them of his presence. The laughter and the singing stopped immediately, and presently three ladies came into sight, looking cautiously in his direction.

Darcy stepped forward. "Miss Bennet. Miss Lucas. I see you are here to enjoy the pleasant weather. Do you come to Oakham Mount often?"

Miss Bennet curtseyed. "My friend is visiting me, and we have come to recover memories of our childhood. Allow me to introduce Miss Clapp, who is here from Southampton."

He bowed solemnly. "Pleased to meet you, Miss Clapp. I hope your childhood memories were all pleasant."

"Very much so, Mr. Darcy."

"We used to roll down that slope, there," said Elizabeth, pointing. "Then we would get into trouble for getting mud on our clothes."

Darcy smiled as he noticed the rim of her petticoat. "It may be ungentlemanly to point it out, but I see little has changed."

Elizabeth looked down ruefully, following the line of his vision, a twinkle in her eye. "It is indeed very unkind of you to draw attention to it. Some things have definitely changed, besides. I would never consider rolling down the slope now."

He chuckled. "Perhaps if I had not been here, you might have been tempted."

The three women protested loudly.

"I am not such a hoyden as that, Mr. Darcy, I can assure you."

He loved that he could joke with her without fearing that she would take offence. He watched her face, mesmerized by the spark in her eyes. She had a way of curling her lips that created small dimples, just there, at bottom of her cheeks. He did not care why she was laughing, but he wanted to laugh with her because it drew him out of his gloom and into a world where happiness and lightness were possible. When he was with her, the past melted away and he could live in the now, in the present.

He felt a stab of envy at her carefree life. She did not have anything in her past to regret. She did not have guilt preying on her mind every day of her life. Her conscience was clear. What he would give to go back to the days when he, too, was not faced with the terrible burden of the past!

What would she say if he told her everything? How would she react? The moment he thought of it, he felt an overwhelming need to confess. Only the fear that she might think he was a monster held him back.

He wanted her to know the truth, but he could not. He would never get a chance to speak to her alone, and even if he did, he did not know her well enough to simply tell her the story of his life, much as he longed to.

Perhaps the first step was to become better acquainted with her.

"Would you care to walk ahead, Miss Bennet? I wanted to show you my favorite view from up here."

She quirked her brow in surprise, then nodded.

"Of course."

As they walked side by side, he was fully aware of how close she was to him. All it would take was to reach out his hand and he be able to touch her. He shut his eyes, mastering the instinct to do so.

"Well, Mr. Darcy? If you continue walking with your eyes shut, you are in danger of rolling down the slope, albeit accidentally."

He opened his eyes, embarrassed at being caught.

"Then I have you to thank for saving me from such an undesirable fate."

She stopped suddenly and pointed above them.

"That, Mr. Darcy, is one of *my* favorite sights."

Darcy looked up. A red kite was gliding above them, its forked tail twisting as it turned, its chestnut feathers the color of Miss Bennet's hair.

"I know many people think of them as pests, but I find them amazingly graceful in flight. Their wings are so elegantly shaped."

Darcy, who shared the idea that kites were pests because they fed on sheep, did not quite know quite what to say. He resorted to silence.

"I see that you do not agree. Or perhaps I am boring you."

"You may be many things, Miss Bennet, but I would not describe you as boring."

"Then how would you describe me?" There was a saucy challenge on her face.

He had fallen right into that one. How would he describe her? Bewitching. Tantalizing. Clever and mischievous. A female Puck. A woodland elf.

He could not say any of these things to her, of course.

"I think you are inquisitive." It was the first neutral word that popped into his head. Even as he said it, he saw how utterly inane it was.

She chuckled. "Ah. I take it you are referring to my interest in Cornwall."

He laughed, amazed as always at the way her mind made connections so rapidly. "Of course. What else?"

∞ ∞ ∞

His laugh startled her. It was full, masculine and deep. When he laughed, his eyes softened and he seemed like another person. How could someone be so different from one moment to the next? When the shadows in his face dissolved, he was very handsome. With the arrogance gone and the tense lines slipping from around his eyes, he looked ten years younger. This Mr. Darcy was a very different one from the one she had known so far.

What was it that haunted him, and made him aloof and solitary? Whatever his past must be, it clearly weighed down upon him. She did not believe what they said about him in Meryton. She had heard rumors, of course. Some said that he had ravished a young lady and abandoned her to her fate, and that her father was in hot pursuit, but she could not quite believe it. She was no judge, of course, but he did not seem to her the type to seduce a young lady. There was no pretense in him. Despite his unwillingness to talk about his past – perhaps even because of his unwillingness to talk about his past – she had the feeling he was by nature an honest person. If he was a villain, she thought, he would have invented a convincing story and would not have hidden in obscurity.

She had found it hard to fathom why someone as open and cheerful as Mr. Bingley would want to be Mr. Darcy's friend. Now she could see there was another side to his character.

Of course, Mr. Bingley was much more agreeable and good natured, she thought, her mind turning once again to the puzzle of Mr. Bingley's departure. She still did not believe he had meant to deceive her, but she could not for the life of her think of a reason for him to have left without saying goodbye. Who better to ask than Mr. Darcy? She was tired of avoiding the issue. She would rather confront it head-on.

"Have you heard from Mr. Bingley by any chance, Mr. Darcy? Has he set a date to return?"

The laughter left Mr. Darcy face, and part of her regretted it, but it was important for her to find out what she could. Her future was at stake.

"Mr. Bingley is a man of impulse," said Darcy, after a long pause. "He tends to make decisions quite suddenly. It is likely he will appear as suddenly as he left."

She frowned. Mr. Bingley himself had said something like this on more than one occasion, but surely no one could be so impulsive, so irresponsible, and certainly not a friend of Mr. Darcy's, who weighed every word and every action of his so carefully.

"Even if his departure was nothing more than a whim, he could still have let his friends know that he was leaving. Perhaps he had not intended to stay away for so long."

"Perhaps."

Mr. Darcy's voice had no inflection.

Elizabeth was starting to feel frustrated at the way he always managed to avoid giving an answer.

She pressed him further. "Perhaps *you* could write and ask when he intends to return? I would if I could, but it would be considered improper."

"You could write to Miss Bingley or Mrs. Hurst."

Her lips curled. "I doubt either of the ladies would be very forthcoming. Besides, I don't know them well enough."

"It is not my place to pressure him."

She was tired of his enigmatic statements. "What does that mean? How can a simple query be perceived as pressure?"

Mr. Darcy shook his head. "I do not think he should feel obliged to return if he does not want to."

"Is that the situation, then? Does he not wish to return?"

"I cannot speak for Mr. Bingley and you must not ask me to, Miss Bennet."

He was looking unhappy again. She felt sorry for hounding him. After all, it wasn't his fault that Mr. Bingley had disappeared so abruptly.

"I must be on my way."

"Goodbye Mr. Darcy."

She curtseyed. He bowed, a dark curl falling endearingly on his face.

"Miss Lucas. Miss Clapp."

He took his leave and moved with a long, determined stride away from them. Elizabeth watched him until he disappeared over the top, realizing only now that he had not shown her his favorite view as he had promised.

∞ ∞ ∞

"Now, Lizzy," said Miss Clapp, as soon as Mr. Darcy was out of earshot. "You have deceived me entirely."

Elizabeth turned to stare at her friend. "Deceived you? Whatever do you mean, Ruth?"

"You led me to believe that Mr. Darcy was very taciturn and unfriendly. Instead, I discover he is flirting with you."

"Flirting? With me? You are completely mistaken, Ruth. Mr. Darcy does not flirt."

Miss Clapp clapped her hands in delight. "That is not what I saw." She looked at Maria. "Don't you think Mr. Darcy was flirting, Maria?"

Maria looked confused. "I thought he was more friendly than usual, and he certainly talked a great deal. I would not go so far as to call it flirting, however."

Miss Clapp gave Elizabeth a knowing look. "You may deny it, Lizzy, but I wasn't born yesterday. Not only was Mr. Darcy flirting with you, but you were flirting back."

Elizabeth burst into laughter. "Now I know you are funning me. The very idea, Ruth! Have you forgotten that I am hoping for Mr. Bingley to return and marry me? You know I am playful with everyone. I think you have been away too long and have forgotten what I am like."

"You will not throw me off the scent, Miss Eliza Bennet."

Just then there was a rumble of thunder and the young ladies looked up in alarm.

"We had better continue this argument someone else," said Elizabeth. "I for one do not wish to be soaked." She picked up her skirts and began to run as the first raindrops began to fall.

∞ ∞ ∞

Darcy returned to Netherfield struggling with a mix of emotions. His encounter with Miss Bennet had awakened in him something he had never felt before. Everything around him seemed sharper, more intense, but at the same time, he felt almost light-headed. He wanted to savor everything about the afternoon. He flung open the window and gazed out across the fields and the tenants' houses towards Oakham Mount. Miss Bennet had stood there, with a light breeze rustling her skirts and pulling at the ribbons of her hat as if trying to remove it. Darcy had been sorely tempted to undo them, tuck his hand under her chin and turn her face towards him.

If only he could indulge himself in these feelings! Why could nothing ever be simple?

Because the facts were staring him in the face, even if his every instinct refused to believe them. Even thinking about Miss Bennet meant betraying his friend, who had sworn to return and claim her.

Besides, it was clear that Miss Bennet's thoughts revolved around Bingley, not around him. She had been most insistent in questioning Darcy about his return. Now, recalling her questions, he felt torn by guilt. Did he have the right to prevent her from marrying a gentleman who had so much to offer her? Setting aside the comfortable life she would gain, there was also the fact that Bingley had the sweetest temperament, was generous to a fault, and was likely to make any woman who married him very happy.

Darcy did not doubt that he had done Bingley a good turn by saving him from a match that would lessen his chances of acceptance into the upper ranks of society. To escape the stigma of trade, Bingley needed to marry a well-bred young lady of impeccable blood. Bingley's father had wanted that for his son and had done everything within his reach to accomplish it.

Which brought him to the real problem. Did he have the right to put his friend's interest above that of Miss Elizabeth Bennet? What if she felt a genuine affection for Bingley? Appearances did not suggest that she was pining for him. On the contrary, she was laughing and singing with her friends and was as animated as she always was. However, that could easily be explained. She expected Bingley to return. She was anxious, true, but she was not worried that she would never see him again. She gave no sign of doubting that he *would* come back.

Darcy could have told her that, if Bingley had one general fault, it was in the constancy of his affections. She would not be the first young lady who had been disappointed when Bingley's attentions had turned elsewhere. His impulsive nature had created tangles often enough. He would believe himself madly in love, but then something or someone else would distract him, and the young lady would find herself forgotten as quickly as she had been taken up. There was no malice in Bingley, and no dissembling. He would never harm anyone nor set out to seduce a young lady. He simply was too impatient to settle on anyone or anything for too long.

Only, in this case, Bingley had not chosen to move away himself. He had agreed to leave reluctantly. Yes, he had been open to persuasion, but if it had been up to him, he would have been engaged to Miss Bennet by now.

Darcy's conscience was twisting and turning, struggling inside him. How could he possibly claim he cared about Miss Bennet, when, by advising his friend to leave, he had not taken Miss Bennet's happiness into consideration at all?

Chapter 15

*M*iss Clapp teased Elizabeth unmercifully during the rest of her visit, and Elizabeth consequently did everything she could to avoid any further encounter with Mr. Darcy. Much as she liked Ruth, her friend's constant insinuations bothered her. She felt Ruth no longer knew her as well as she used to. How could anyone possibly think Elizabeth had an interest in Mr. Darcy, of all people, when the whole world knew her only interest was Mr. Bingley?

Nevertheless, she was sorry when Miss Clapp left, and, no sooner had she left, when Elizabeth wished Ruth back in Meryton. By now she was feeling Bingley's absence more keenly. It had been several weeks since he had left, and she was beginning to have moments when she wondered if he would ever return.

She felt this particularly keenly one evening, especially since she had no one to confide in. She could not talk about her fears over Mr. Bingley to Maria, who would mention it to Lady Lucas, who in turn would take pleasure in the failure of Elizabeth's hopes. With no one else to confide in, Elizabeth sat down to write a letter to Charlotte Collins.

Dear Charlotte,

I apologize for my delay in writing. You asked me to keep you informed about Mr. Bingley's return, but so far, I have nothing new to report. *Unfortunately, there is no sign of him yet, and I am beginning to wonder whether he has abandoned me! However, it is too gloomy to allow myself to think this way and I will continue to expect him until, finally, when I am old and withered, I will realise that there is no chance of his returning.*

Meanwhile, you will never guess who came to visit. Ruth Clapp! However, her visit was quite ruined for me by her insistence that I was flirting with Mr. Darcy! I fear Ruth has completely forgotten my playful nature, and is judging me by entirely new standards. However, I will admit one thing. He is more handsome than Mr. Bingley. There, I have said it. Now condemn me if you will!

We continue to discover nothing about Mr. Darcy, who is as tight-lipped as ever about his past, though I admit he has grown less arrogant and easier to talk to than I would have expected.

I have no other news, except to tell you that papa has recovered completely, and is enjoying his hunting as much as the other gentlemen. I believe he will be hunting with Mr. Darcy tomorrow. I wonder if Mr. Darcy will stay for dinner? He generally does not.

I will write to you again when the long-awaited arrival of Mr. Bingley happens. Meanwhile, I hope all is well with Baby William, and that Mr. Collins continues to dote on him.

With all my good wishes,

Your friend, Elizabeth

Elizabeth read the letter and folded it, satisfied that it expressed what was needed. It was at times like this that Elizabeth missed

Charlotte's quiet intelligence, and, although she had condemned her friend's practical approach to marriage, she had since come to appreciate her common sense a great deal.

Still there was no denying her relationship was much more strained than it used to be. Elizabeth could not forget the worry she had suffered when papa had been ill, and the knowledge that Charlotte could easily have taken her place.

She put her hands between her face. Although her father was safe now, she was more aware than ever of the need for an advantageous marriage. If only Mr. Bingley would return!

∞ ∞ ∞

After Ruth Clapp's departure, Elizabeth ran into Mr. Darcy on several occasions in Meryton, and they stopped to talk briefly before they each continued on their way. The two also met once again at Lucas Lodge and at Aunt Phillip's. On each occasion, Elizabeth enquired about Mr. Bingley, but Darcy had no news from him. Still, Mr. Darcy always managed to draw her into conversation. He would enquire about a book she had read, or about an item in the newspaper, and they would fall into a lively discussion. He had a quick mind, she discovered, and was not entirely devoid of humor.

Mrs. Bennet, however, continued to dislike him, and to discourage her from talking to him, and to bemoan the absence of his friend.

"Why couldn't Mr. Darcy have left us for London, instead of Mr. Bingley? I cannot stand the sight of him, but I suppose we must continue to endure his presence. Let us hope Mr. Bingley comes back soon."

Elizabeth did not try to change Mrs. Bennet's opinion. In any case, everyone missed Mr. Bingley, including her, so there was nothing to argue about there.

But as winter drew to a close, and the first signs of spring appeared, it became evident that Mr. Bingley was in no hurry to return. The longer Mr. Bingley stayed away, the more Elizabeth became the object of pity, and Mrs. Bennet began to become quite agitated whenever Mr. Bingley's name came up.

"I really don't know why everyone keeps asking me about Mr. Bingley this and Mr. Bingley that. I am quite sick of Mr. Bingley. I wish he had never come. If Mr. Bingley does not intend to return to Netherfield, I wish he would make up his mind and lease out Netherfield, to give the opportunity to another young man to take his place."

"Mama, how can you wish such a thing? For all you know, Mr. Bingley could return within a week."

"Well, Lizzy, you must not take offence if anyone criticizes your Mr. Bingley. He has behaved very badly indeed. To take off like that without so much as a by-your-leave! You cannot forever find excuses for him."

"I am not finding excuses." Elizabeth, too, had lost her patience with Mr. Bingley. All it would have taken was a letter from his sister to clarify matters, but neither he nor his sisters had made the least effort to keep anyone informed.

"I hope he doesn't come back," said Lydia one morning, as she was trimming yet another hat. "Think how thrilling it would be for us all to have a new handsome neighbor."

"What if he was not handsome at all, but an old man with warts and ten children?"

"Don't be ridiculous, Lizzy," said Mrs. Bennet. "Why should he have ten children, when we have just had an eligible gentleman like Mr. Bingley?"

Elizabeth snapped off the end of a thread between her teeth and stuck her needle into the pin cushion. "Much use it did anyone."

"Just because you failed to capture him, Lizzy," said Lydia, "it doesn't mean no one else could have. If you'd left him to me, and not been so selfish, it might have ended differently."

The twisted logic of Lydia's statement was too much for Elizabeth's dampened spirits.

"I don't see when you are all so certain that Mr. Bingley won't be returning." She put down her sewing and jumped to her feet. "I think I shall go for a walk."

Kitty was humming as she embroidered a cushion. She looked up, and, seeing that Elizabeth was looking red in the face, said kindly, "Perhaps Mr. Bingley may return after all, and bring with him another party from London."

Everyone seemed to find that idea appealing, and the prospect of a new tenant was forgotten. Elizabeth took advantage of their preoccupation to leave the room and fetch her spencer. She needed time to herself, away from the constant company of her family. Even though there was a cold wind blowing, a brisk walk was exactly what she needed to consider how she felt about Mr. Bingley's absence.

∞ ∞ ∞

It was a risk setting up a meeting here, or anywhere else for that matter, thought Darcy uneasily, but he had been unable to resist meeting up with his cousin Richard after all this time. Richard had been summoned to Rosings to consult with Lady Catherine on some business, and since his cousin would be traveling south not too far from Meryton, it seemed like a perfect opportunity for them to arrange a meeting. Darcy desperately wanted news of Georgiana and Pemberley, and he was certain that even a few hours in his cousin's company would go a long way to satisfying his yearning for home.

They had decided on this particular inn, the Spotted Dog, for two reasons. The first was that it was about halfway between The Great North Road and Meryton, and a reasonable ride for both of them. The second was that it was not on any of the major thoroughfares, which minimized the possibility of travelers. Richard had chosen the place after making several enquiries. It was a quiet village inn and, even if two strangers might arouse curiosity, it was off the beaten track. If they went during the day, when things were quiet, there would be even less chance of any unwanted encounters.

Richard Fitzwilliam was waiting for Darcy when he entered. The welcome sight of his cousin's dear familiar face brought a lump to Darcy's throat. The two embraced, patting each other on the back vigorously.

"You've lost a few hairs since I last saw you," said Darcy, laughing.

Fitzwilliam ran his hand through his thick locks. "I have not lost a single hair, Darcy, and well you know it. However, I am sorry to say you have not fared as well as I have. There are quite a few wrinkles around your eyes."

Darcy looked at himself closely in the mirror. "I think you need spectacles, my dear cousin."

They laughed in easy companionship and settled down at the crude wooden table.

"I won't tell Aunt Catherine that we have met. She has been complaining that you haven't visited her since you returned and she seems to take it as a personal insult."

"Doesn't she understand the gravity of the situation?"

Fitzwilliam made a face.

"She believes the servants are too frightened of her to gossip. Of course, she is deluded. Servants always gossip. Besides, even if it was true, all it would take for someone to mention you quite by accident, and the cat would be out of the bag."

They ordered pie and ale and settled down to talk. They were so immersed in conversation that they were unaware of the passage of time until a commotion outside made them aware that the day was coming to an end.

"I had better go," said Darcy. "I do not want to risk a fall because I did not see a pothole in the road."

The noise outside the private parlor had grown threefold and it became clear that the inn was not at all the quiet place they had imagined. As they stepped out of the private room, it became apparent that they had chosen an unfortunate day to meet. From the volume of betting that was happening, the names of the animals, and the crowing sounds that came from the back room, everything indicated that there was going to be a cock fight. Darcy and Fitzwilliam raised the collars of their great coats and made their way slowly through the crowd, trying to hide their faces. Darcy kept his head down and lowered his top hat to conceal his identity the best he could.

As they stepped outside into the growing dusk, Richard gave a sigh of relief. "I'm not made for this cloak and dagger stuff, Darcy."

"Neither am I, but needs must." He put out his hand. "We shouldn't linger. Give my greetings to Georgiana."

As they waited for the horses to be saddled, neither of the two gentlemen noticed the man standing in the shadows, watching them.

∞ ∞ ∞

Elizabeth was about to set out for Meryton to return a book to the circulating library when a letter arrived for her. She immediately recognized the writing as Charlotte's. The weather being pleasant outdoors, she sat on a bench to read it, anticipating some amusing anecdotes related to Lady Catherine.

As she began to read it, however, a dull, heavy sensation came over her.

Dear Lizzy,

I have news that will surprise you very much. Remember I told you that Lady Catherine's nephew, Colonel Fitzwilliam, would be coming to visit his aunt? Usually he comes during Easter, but this year Lady Catherine summoned him for some urgent estate business. But I digress. Well, I discovered the most astonishing thing. I am almost certain that your Mr. Darcy is his cousin!

I would never have suspected it, if it had not been for a conversation I overheard when I was invited to dine at Rosings. Mr. Collins and I had just arrived and were being taken in by the butler. He was just about to announce us, when I overheard Lady Catherine (you know how her voice carries!) complaining about her nephew Darcy. She said she understood him failing to visit her when he was abroad, but she was most put out by the fact that Darcy had not come to see her since his return. Colonel Fitzwilliam mentioned "his situation," but Lady

Catherine said that he could not keep hiding away forever. It was time for him to face the guns.

I may have had some doubt that the two were the same person, but then I heard the word 'Meryton' mentioned. So, putting two and two together, I have little doubt that your Mr. Darcy and Lady Catherine's nephew are one and the same!

You may think that this is more than enough news, but there is more to come. Later in the evening, Lady Catherine returned to the topic of the colonel's "cousin." She was careful not to mention his name, but she asked whether his cousin was cast down by his situation. The colonel replied that he was in good spirits, and that, even in his restricted circumstances, he had just performed a good deed for a friend. According to the colonel, Mr. Darcy saved his friend from a disastrous mistake. This friend was intent on a precipitous marriage into a most unfortunate family, but Darcy had managed to put a stop to it at the very last moment.

I can only conclude that the friend being referred to was Mr. Bingley, and that you finally have the explanation for Mr. Bingley's sudden departure.

I will not write more as I want to send this express so you may receive the news as soon as posssible.

Ever your friend,

Charlotte Collins

Elizabeth's hands trembled, and the letter slipped from her fingers and tumbled to the ground. So it was Mr. Darcy who had convinced Mr. Bingley to leave! The revelation made the blood in her veins run cold. Yet he had pretended to be Elizabeth's friend! He had spoken to her almost intimately. She had confided in him when papa was sick, had trusted him, and all the time, he was doing everything he could to destroy her happiness! He had betrayed her, completely and utterly. She would never forgive him.

Her mind went back to the first day when she had met Mr. Darcy at the Meryton Assembly. Her first impressions of him had been right. His arrogance and contempt had been apparent from the first moment. She had instinctively been repelled by his superior attitude, and his insult to her had sealed her dislike of him. Somehow, along the way, she had not only forgiven him, but had come to see him far more sympathetically than she ought to. She thought of the night when he had taken her home when her father was so ill. He had been so gentle, almost tender. Was that all a sham? She had turned to him instinctively for help. He had repaid her trust in him by turning Mr. Bingley away from her and destroying any possibility of a relationship between them.

What possible objection could Mr. Darcy have to a marriage between her and Mr. Bingley? If anything, the marriage would be disadvantageous to her. She was the daughter of a gentleman, while Bingley was the son of a tradesman. In what way did he consider her family inferior to Bingley's?

The more she thought about it, the angrier she became, and the stronger the sense of betrayal she felt. She began to march up and down the garden, but soon was unable to bear its confines. She had to get away from prying eyes; she did not want mama to ask her about the letter. She decided to go for a vigorous walk, hoping to find some calm.

She would not let him get away with it, she decided. She would confront him, the first opportunity she had.

∞ ∞ ∞

Mr. Darcy set out to Meryton in search of Miss Bennet. It was a beautiful day, with snowdrops and crocuses heralding the beginning of spring. The hedges were dotted with white blossoms, and the birds were busy hurrying back and forth to build their nests. Darcy was feeling at peace with the world. His encounter with his cousin had brought some relief to his isolation, and he began to see that he need not be as cut off from the world as he had earlier believed.

Bingley was showing no signs of returning. He need not concern himself with that aspect of things. It was difficult for Miss Bennet, of course, but clearly Bingley had already forgotten her. Eventually, she would realize that he was not going to return, and Darcy would be there to help her recover.

What good would that do? Every time he reached this point in his thoughts, he found himself facing the same issue. He had spent many a night agonizing over it. How could he marry anyone when he had to live in hiding every day of his life?

There had to be a solution. He would find a way for them to be together. He could set up his own house near Longbourn. Everyone here knew him, and Miss Bennet would not have to leave her friends and acquaintances. They would be unable to travel anywhere, of course, but she rarely travelled in any case.

But first, of course, he would have to find a way to reveal his past to her. How he would accomplish that, he had no idea. The very idea of exposing his inner self to her reduced him to incoherence. Perhaps if he wrote things down – if he wrote everything in a letter – it was highly improper, but it was the only way.

He stopped in Meryton to buy some parchment paper and some new ink and set out with the parcel tucked under his arm, eager to begin.

To his delight, as he passed Clarke's library, he saw that Miss Bennet was moving in that direction. He thanked providence that he had not lingered in the shop or he would have missed her. He wished he had picked some crocuses earlier to give to her, but it was too late now.

"Miss Bennet. Well met. Are you going in to borrow a book? I will join you, if I may."

"I cannot talk, sir. I am rather in a hurry."

She was sounding breathless, and her voice was cold. She looked pale, as well. Darcy felt a pinch of alarm.

"Is there something wrong, Miss Bennet? Has someone taken ill?"

She did not answer and continued to hurry onwards. He did not want to leave, especially if there was something troubling her.

She stopped suddenly and turned to him. "I will not walk any further with you, Mr. Darcy. It is improper for a young lady to walk unaccompanied with a single gentleman."

He expected her to laugh, but she was completely serious, and she was avoiding his gaze. Her face, usually so expressive, was closed against him. He felt bewildered.

"I am sure no one can accuse you of impropriety, Miss Bennet. You have everyone's respect, including my own."

Her eyebrow arched. "Really, Mr. Darcy? You need not pretend any longer. I know the truth."

Her words slammed into him with the force of a blow. He felt the blood drain from his face. So she had discovered what he had done. No wonder she did not want anything further to do with him. She would shun him, as everyone in the vicinity would do.

He stood completely still, vaguely aware of a bird singing in a tree above him, his thoughts scattered in a hundred directions, trying to come to terms with this. He had not expected her to judge him so harshly. And to think he had been on the verge of uncovering to her his innermost thoughts, that he had planned to let her see his naked soul.

"I know your opinion of me," she said, her hands locked behind her back. "You made it abundantly clear when you advised Mr. Bingley to abandon me."

His jumbled thoughts took a moment to catch up with her words. He stood there, stunned, realizing she was talking, not about his past, but about something else entirely. Relief gave way to dismay. He looked away. Now he was the one who was unable to meet her gaze. All the guilt he had been feeling was showing on his face, he was sure of it. He felt overheated and he put his hand on his cravat in a futile attempt to loosen it.

"We welcomed you into our homes, even if we didn't know who you were. We trusted you and treated you as one of our own, yet all the time you have been stabbing us in the back. You have stabbed *me* in the back by deliberately coming between me and Mr. Bingley. How could you do such a thing?"

He did not know what to say. He needed to think. How could he explain himself without further insulting her?

"Do you deny it, Mr. Darcy?" Her eyes were flashing with anger.

In spite of everything, in spite of the direness of his situation, all he could think of was how beautiful she looked.

"I suppose you did not think I would ever find out. You have been talking to me as if you respected my opinion, but now I know you look at me with contempt. Did you think I could continue my acquaintance with someone who has destroyed my chance of happiness, perhaps forever?"

He did not look at her with contempt. Far from it. His heart cried out in protest. "Miss Bennet—"

"You think yourself so far above me, so superior. But you have behaved in such an ungentlemanly manner that I am not certain you deserve the name. You conduct leaves me with no choice but to withdraw my friendship."

Her words snapped like a whip in the air, sharp and final. "Goodbye, Mr. Darcy."

She walked away.

His heart clenched tight like a fist. He began to stumble in the opposite direction, half blind, scarcely knowing what he was doing.

The man who was the means of destroying my happiness.

She loved Bingley. He did not doubt it now. The depth of her feelings – he would never forget the quivering of her lips, the single tear that had escaped from the corner of her eye. She had brushed it impatiently aside, but he had seen it.

He had caused Elizabeth the most profound unhappiness. He was nothing more than a scoundrel. She was right, even if she was mistaken about his opinion of her. He understood now why he had sent Bingley away. It was because he wanted her for himself.

There, he had said it, but now there was no mistaking the stark reality. He had fallen in love for the first time in his life. He should have rejoiced in the matter, but there was no reason for joy, no reason to hope. Miss Bennet was not in love with him. She was in love with Bingley. She wanted Bingley. Her tears, the despair he had witnessed – they were all the evidence he needed.

Even if she cared for him, which clearly she did not, he had nothing to offer her, nothing at all. He was a fugitive, with no home, and no future. And why should she care about him? He had made two people unhappy to satisfy his own needs.

He was flooded with self-loathing, remorse, and regret. Of course he deserved everything she said and more. He had nothing to say to her, beyond telling her he was sorry.

The future, which had seemed so hopeful just a short time ago, had now turned to ashes.

Chapter 16

*E*lizabeth walked away quickly. He could see her agitation in every step she took. As she stepped into the road to cross the other side, Darcy realized she had not seen the danger hurtling towards her. The stage coach, packed with travelers and with a fresh team of horses, was almost upon her, two pairs of horses galloping relentlessly onward. With a cry of warning, he flew across the space between them and knocked her sideways. She toppled to the ground and he threw himself against her, protecting her from the horse's hooves, covering every inch of her.

The stage coach thundered by, never pausing, with inches to spare.

The terror of what might have happened left him shaking. It was a miracle that she had not been hurt. The breath had been knocked out of him by the impact of their fall, and for a long moment he just lay there, trying to get his breath back.

As his heartbeat slowed, Darcy became conscious that Elizabeth's warm body lay beneath him. A surge of desire rose up in him, flooding him with sensations that rammed into him with a force that matched that of the stage coach. Elizabeth's face was inches from his own, her sweet lips parted as if awaiting him.

He forgot about the world around them and bent his face towards her. In that moment nothing mattered but the urgent need to kiss her.

"Miss Bennet? Are you injured?" A man's voice reached him. There were other voices, too, murmurs and gasps and indrawn breaths.

The voices were like a slosh of frozen water. They took him from a dream world back to cold reality. He jerked upwards, tearing himself painfully from her touch.

"Are you injured, Miss Bennet?" he said in a voice he barely recognized as his own. It occurred to him that she had not uttered a sound. She was still lying on the ground, not moving.

With alarm, he berated himself for thinking of kissing her when she might be suffering a broken limb or rib or some other painful injury. His weight must have crushed her. He pulled himself to a kneeling position and looked around him. A small crowd was gathered around them. Embarrassment and chagrin brought him to full awareness. He had almost kissed her in the middle of Meryton!

He reached out to help her up, worried now. She still hadn't said anything.

"Miss Bennet?"

She stirred and slowly began to move. Worry turned to relief as she put out her hand to him.

"Poor thing," said a woman who had pushed her way to the front. "She's in shock. Bring her to the shop, Mr. Darcy, and I'll give her some sweet tea. She'll need a few minutes to recover herself."

He helped Miss Bennet to stand up and gave her his arm to lean on. She held onto it lightly, keeping her distance, walking stiffly.

He moved slowly, in case she had hurt something. She was limping a little, but mercifully she showed no signs of anything serious.

Her gloved hand burned into his skin, in spite of the layers of cloth that separated them. He tried to keep his distance, aware that every move of his was being observed.

It was slow, but they gradually reached the milliner's shop and he helped her sit down.

The milliner fussed about and sent one of her girls to make tea in the back. There was really nothing for him to do here. The shop was small, and there was only one chair.

"I will go to the inn and bring a carriage to take Miss Bennet home," he said. "I can see she is in safe hands."

As he walked out, he noticed for the first time the aches and pains in his body. The wound in his shoulder hurt. His wrist had been jolted when he landed on the ground, and one of his ribs was sore. There would be a bruise or two, but he welcomed them fiercely. He had saved Miss Bennet from danger, and that was what mattered.

∞ ∞ ∞

Darcy hurried to the George and Hounds to secure a conveyance to take Miss Bennet home. She appeared unharmed, but that was only because the shock had not yet worn off. The sooner he could take her home, the better.

As he entered the inn, he went straight to the innkeeper and ordered someone sent to the apothecary to attend Miss Bennet in Longbourn. Then he requested a carriage to be prepared.

"I'm afraid I only have a dog-cart available, Mr. Darcy." The innkeeper looked apologetic.

A dog-cart would fit Darcy's purposes perfectly. It was an open carriage and would not require a chaperon. Unfortunately, it would be cold.

"That will have to do. Make sure to have some bricks warmed, then."

The innkeeper hurried off to give his orders. He knew Mr. Darcy, since he and Mr. Bingley had dined at the inn at least once a week in the first weeks of their arrival.

"Mr. Darcy?"

Darcy went very still. The man addressing him was a stranger, which would have been enough to worry Darcy, but his tone left no doubt that he knew exactly who Darcy was.

As the man stepped into the light, Darcy recognized him. The last time he had seen him, he had been laughing and drunk.

"Hollins."

"I see you remember me. Good. That will make matters easier. I suggest you request a private parlor where we can have a conversation."

Darcy thought of Elizabeth, who was waiting for the carriage. "I'm afraid I have no time for you at present."

He strode towards the door. The man put out a leg to trip him up, and, as Darcy stumbled, Hollins' hand shot out to grasp him.

"Not so fast, Mr. Darcy. I have no intention of allowing you to escape."

"I have no intention of escaping," said Darcy, between tight lips, "I have an urgent errand to fulfil. Kindly let me go."

"I'm afraid I can't do that."

Darcy considered punching the man in the face, but already people's faces were turned in their direction, and the last thing he wanted to do was draw attention.

"I give you my word I will return," said Darcy.

"I don't care a fig for your word." The man sneered. "Ask for the private parlor now, sir, or I'm afraid I will have to inform those fine gentlemen over there exactly who you are and what you have done."

Darcy seethed with frustration, but he had no choice, and he knew it. "Very well, Hollins. Whatever it is, make it quick."

Hollins gave a satisfied smile. "I knew you'd come round to my way of thinking."

The innkeeper had returned by now. "The cart is ready, Mr. Darcy."

"Have someone else take Miss Bennet home. She is at the milliner's. I have a meeting. Please bring us drinks in a private parlor."

If the innkeeper was surprised at Darcy's sudden request for a private room, he gave no indication.

"Bring us the best port you have," said Hollins, in an amiable tone.

The moment the door closed, Darcy leaned against it, refusing to sit down.

"Spit it out, man. Say what you have to say."

Darcy already had a good idea what Hollins would have to say, but there was no getting around listening to him.

"Now, now, what's the hurry? We can reach an agreement over port like gentlemen. No need to stand on ceremony."

Darcy growled. "*You* may drink the port, but I have no intention of sharing it. Get on with it."

Hollins sat down and put his boots up on the table, settling in comfortably.

"The fact is, Mr. Darcy, I was owed a great deal of money from a certain party we both know – gambling debts, debts of honor, that sort of thing. Due to circumstances that you are well aware of, I was never paid back."

"Circumstances have nothing to do with it. If you knew Wickham well enough, you would know he rarely paid his debts. He owed money to a great many people."

"Tut, tut, Mr. Darcy. Is that how you speak of someone who was practically your brother?"

"It is the truth, and well you know it."

"The *truth*, sir, is not something that would serve you very well. In fact, I would be willing to bet a thousand guineas that you would not like *Miss Bennet* to know the truth." Hollins watched Darcy closely to see how he would receive this. Darcy kept his expression under tight control, revealing nothing.

Hollins poured himself some port. "Now, I'm a reasonable man, Mr. Darcy, and I don't hold grudges. If you could see it in yourself to pay me what was owed to me by Mr. Wickham, we can forget I have ever seen you, and allow bygones to be bygones."

Darcy knew exactly what kind of man Hollins was. He did not have an honorable bone in his body. If he gave in to him once, the blackmail would never cease, and Hollins would bleed him dry.

He felt a profound sadness, knowing that Hollins was also the type of man who would try to extract a reward for revealing his location. Darcy had been happy here and had been able to forget for a brief time the terrible burden of the past. Now, however, his sojourn in this quiet area of the countryside was over.

"I'm afraid I can't help you, Hollins." His tone was cold as ice.

The relaxed, easy demeanor disappeared as Hollins sprang to his feet.

"Now, then, Mr. Darcy, I don't think you realize quite how much trouble you are in. I can go to the authorities this very moment and give them the information for your arrest."

"On the contrary, Hollins, I know exactly what you are capable of. Unfortunately, there is nothing I can do about it. I have no intention of wasting my money trying to prevent something that is bound to happen anyway."

Hollins saw the opportunity to make money slipping quickly through his fingers.

He smiled. It was an ugly smile, full of malice. "I'll ask you one more time, Mr. Darcy, very nicely. It's your last chance. Otherwise..." He drew very close to Darcy in a threatening manner, and made the sign of a hangman's noose.

Darcy had had enough of Hollins' leering face. He did what he had wanted to do the moment he'd first set eyes on him. His fist went out and connected with his jaw. Hollins staggered backwards, then, recovering his footing, lunged towards him.

Darcy had not survived the Peninsular Campaign without learning a few things about defending himself. He sidestepped, allowing Hollins to crash into the door. He then took hold of him by the back of his coat and tossed him to the ground.

Hollins put a hand to his nose, which was bleeding.

"You're going to regret this, Darcy."

"I already regret everything about this encounter." He took out his purse and threw some coins on the table. "I suggest you clean up and finish the brandy. You don't want it to go to waste."

And with that, he straightened his clothes, opened the door and stalked out.

∞ ∞ ∞

Darcy walked out of the inn with his thoughts in turmoil. Part of him hoped Hollins was calling his bluff, but it was unlikely. He had seen the malice in Hollins' eyes. Besides, he was still hoping to make money from Darcy's predicament by asking for a reward. As far as Darcy knew, there was no reward attached to his arrest, but it was possible they would give him something.

He passed by the milliner's shop. The woman there assured him that Miss Bennet had not suffered any unpleasant effects from the incident, and that she had been taken home by an outrider from the George and Hounds.

Darcy paid the milliner for the tea and thanked her for her assistance, then continued on his way.

∞ ∞ ∞

The walk to Netherfield relieved some of his agitation, but it did not diminish the urgency of making a decision. It seemed to him that the wisest course would be to depart for Cornwall at once. He could take a roundabout way so that it would be difficult to trace his direction.

However, he soon thought better of that idea. He had spent so much time telling everyone that he was from Cornwall, that even the most casual enquiry would point in that direction. It was the first place they would look. Meanwhile, he did not want to be waiting in Cornwall expecting someone to find him on a daily basis.

He could go somewhere else entirely, he supposed. His uncle had a hunting lodge in the Scottish Highlands. That should be sufficiently remote to make it difficult to find him. If he did not take the Great North Road – if he travelled by the backroads – he might be able to conceal his direction by stopping only at out of the way inns. It would take him a lot more time, of course, but that did not matter.

He soon talked himself out of that. If anyone received a hint that he was travelling north, they would assume he was going to Pemberley, and they would soon turn up on Georgiana's doorstep. Richard was still at Rosings, and Georgiana would be required to deal with the problem by herself. Even if he himself did not go there, they would make things uncomfortable for her.

In the end, it was clear he had run out of options.

It was time to face the consequences of his actions. He could not continue to hide all his life. He would save the authorities the trouble of coming to arrest him by going to London and handing himself in to await trial.

∞ ∞ ∞

Having made the decision, he felt in many ways relieved. He had dreaded this possibility for so long, but now it was all over. No more looking over his shoulder. No more uncertainty. No more pretending. He could claim his name again.

In any case, there was nothing for him here. He thought of Miss Bennet. She felt nothing but contempt for him, and when she knew what he had done, she would condemn him even more.

He ordered a portmanteau to be prepared with all his essentials, but the thought of what the villagers would think – of what Miss Bennet would think – if he stole away in the dead of night made him hesitate. He considered going to say goodbye to Miss Bennet, but what explanation could he possibly give? He was not prepared at this particular moment to tell her the truth. She already thought badly enough of him.

He grimaced as he recalled the things she had said to him. Saving her from a speeding chaise would not change anything between them. To make matters worse, he was now ashamed of how he had reacted when they were on the ground. He might have kissed her in full view of the whole town! What a mess that would have created!

He seemed incapable of behaving normally when he was around Miss Elizabeth Bennet and, considering that she did not care for him at all, the best thing he could do was to remove himself from her presence, and save himself from constant temptation. Miss Bennet belonged to Bingley, not to him.

Even if she did not care about Bingley, what future could he possibly offer her? He had no future. As Hollins had been kind enough to remind him, his future may well be at the end of a rope.

His options were limited. He had no choice but to leave quickly and confront his demons. One way, or the other, he would find peace.

∞ ∞ ∞

The following morning, the door to the parlor flew open and Lydia rushed in, followed by Kitty.

"I have news! You will never guess what it is." Her eyes gleamed.

Mrs. Bennet sat upright in her chair. "Mr. Bingley has come at last! Oh, I knew it! Make haste, girls. We must invite him for dinner before anyone else."

"No mama, this isn't about Mr. Bingley. It is about Mr. Darcy."

"Oh." Mrs. Bennet's face fell. "Well, I care nothing for news of Mr. Darcy."

"But you must! Mr. Darcy has left Netherfield. He left early this morning with a carriage loaded with trunks. It does not look like he intends to come back."

Mrs. Bennet stared, trying to digest this unexpected turn of events.

"But why? Why did he leave so suddenly?"

Lydia was more than pleased to have evoked such astonishment. "Some are saying that both Mr. Darcy and Bingley were crooks, and that we will soon discover that they have made off with all the china and the silver at Netherfield."

Elizabeth sat in silence, her mind whirling at this turn of events. Could Mr. Darcy have left because she had quarreled with him? Surely not. However, it seemed too great a coincidence for him to leave so soon after their quarrel.

Perhaps it had nothing to do with their quarrel, but rather with the fact that she now knew who he was. As if she would reveal his identity to everyone! He should have known better. Yet it was all very puzzling. Clearly Mr. Darcy did have something to hide, and was worried about Elizabeth revealing his identity.

She had been angry at him yesterday, but now she wanted to talk to him. He had saved her life. At the very least she needed to thank him.

"Good riddance," said Mrs. Bennet. "I have never liked the man. I have always thought there was something sinister about him. No one knows why he was concealing his past. For all we know, he may be a murderer."

Mr. Bennet happened to be passing by at that particular moment.

"Who may be a murderer?"

Mrs. Bennet was pleased to have attracted Mr. Bennet's attention. "Why, Mr. Darcy, of course."

"Mr. Darcy? What an extraordinary idea! You are quite mistaken, madam. I would advise you not to spread rumors and blacken a good man's name."

"A good man? Mr. Darcy? Certainly not." She sniffed. "No one would sneak away the way he did unless he was up to something."

"Allow me to be a better judge of a gentleman's character than you are, my dear."

"Then explain why it is that he has packed and left so suddenly, without a moment's notice? There is something very suspicious in the matter. I do not see how you can defend him. I have never encountered a more disagreeable, haughty man in my life. And to think you invited him to hunt with you! Why, he might even have taken a shot at you."

"However, the fact is, he did not, though he had ample opportunity. Even if what you said was true, Mrs. Bennet, I doubt he would simply go around the countryside killing people for no reason at all." He looked highly amused.

"I see you persist in defending the villain. All I can say is I am very glad he is gone. We can now sleep safely in our beds again."

"I for one have been sleeping very safely in my bed. I am sorry to hear that you have been living in fear all these days, my dear."

"Oh, Mr. Bennet, you are just trying to vex me. But if he had murdered one of us, you would not be talking that way."

"Well, I wish he may have murdered Lydia, then we would have been rid of one of the silliest girls in England."

Chapter 17

*E*lizabeth could not help thinking of everything she had said to Darcy, over and over. She had no idea if she had driven him away, but she regretted saying anything to him. She had provided him with ample evidence of her uncivil upbringing, and had behaved more like a fishmonger than a genteel young lady. She had not even given him a moment to defend himself.

Yet he had saved her life – or at least, saved her from being hurt. She would never really know how close she had been to being hit by the carriage. It had happened so quickly, everything was a blur. It was only afterwards that she had registered what had happened, as the horses' hooves pounded loudly past her.

Even then, she had been distracted by Mr. Darcy's body covering hers. She relived that moment over and over – the sharp masculine scent of him, the feel of his muscles against her, the intimate contact she felt through her clothes. When she thought he was about to kiss her, she had stopped breathing. She had wanted him to do it, to experience the press of his lips against hers. She had never felt anything like this in her life, but then, she had never had such close contact with a man before. She was embarrassed to recall that she had been lost to all propriety at that moment.

She didn't know what to think or feel anymore. She still could hardly believe that he was Mr. Fitzwilliam Darcy of Pemberley, not an insignificant guest of Mr. Bingley's. He was the nephew of an Earl, no less. Small wonder he was so arrogant. Not that Elizabeth approved of his condescending manner, but it could have been worse. He was related to Lady Catherine. Yet compared with her, he was the epitome of good manners. Elizabeth had met that lady on more than one occasion when she had visited Charlotte, and only her sense of humor had prevented her from being insulted by Lady Catherine's rudeness.

Oh, why had she not held her tongue after hearing from Charlotte? Why had she lashed out immediately in that way? She could not excuse herself by saying it was an accident. She had been half-hoping to run into Mr. Darcy – she was spoiling for an encounter. She wanted to confront him about Mr. Bingley. She should have not come out of the house until she had considered the matter at some length.

Now he was gone, unexpectedly, just like Bingley, and without saying goodbye.

She spent the night tossing and turning, her mind so preoccupied it was impossible to sleep. Her mind replayed his words over and over. The next morning, she was like a ghost, entirely drained of emotion.

"Lizzy, are you sickening?" said Mary, as Elizabeth took her seat at the breakfast table.

"Lizzy is sickening because she has lost Mr. Bingley," said Lydia, with a vindictive look. "Now, with Mr. Darcy gone, Mr. Bingley will never return."

"It doesn't matter whether he does or doesn't," Elizabeth replied, firmly. She had reached a decision. "If he does return, I won't be here. I'm planning to go to Town."

"What?" Lydia sat up in her chair and looked at Mrs. Bennet. "If Lizzy's going to London, mama, then I'm going, too."

"And I," echoed Kitty.

"What's this about going to London?" said Mrs. Bennet. "This is the first I hear of it."

"I have decided to go to London, mama, but I will go alone. I will take Penny, of course, or a girl from the village if you can't spare her."

Mrs. Bennet's eyes narrowed. "You're going to find Mr. Bingley."

Elizabeth said nothing.

Mrs. Bennet considered the idea, then nodded. "You're finally doing something sensible. If Mr. Bingley won't come to us, then you must go to him."

"Do I have your permission, papa?"

Mr. Bennet peered at her over his spectacles. "To pursue Mr. Bingley? Are you sure that's wise?"

"I don't want to stay here wondering what happened and not knowing."

He examined her further. She had the feeling he knew there was more to the matter than Mr. Bingley.

"I daresay we will not have any peace until you've had your way, Lizzy. Go then. But don't stay away too long."

"I want to go, too, papa." Lydia had a mulish look on her face.

To Elizabeth's surprise, it was Mrs. Bennet who stepped in. "No. Only Lizzy can go. You will get in her way. Besides, Jane is increasing, and cannot take care of too many guests." As Lydia looked sullen, Mrs. Bennet added. "If Lizzy convinces Mr. Bingley to propose, then I will buy you a new hat."

Mrs. Bennet knew exactly how to distract her daughters. Elizabeth's trip to London was quickly forgotten as they took advantage of the situation to ask for new dresses as well.

Elizabeth stood up to go to her chamber to write an express to Jane, surprised at how quickly everything had been agreed upon. As she passed Mr. Bennet's chair, however, he put a hand on her arm to hold her back.

"Are you entirely certain you wish to marry Mr. Bingley, Lizzy?"

Elizabeth bit her lip. "I am not certain, Papa. But I need to go to London."

Mr. Bennet pushed back his glasses. "I thought so. Well hurry there and come back, then. I will have no one sensible to talk to while you are away."

She smiled. "I am sure you will find plenty of things to amuse you."

His eyes twinkled. "Very true. I wish you luck, Lizzy, whatever it is you are up to."

Three days later, when she was in the carriage on her way, Elizabeth reflected about what she wanted to accomplish in her trip. She had not been entirely honest about her reason for coming to London. It *was* true that she intended to call on the Bingleys, but was it the main reason she was going there? It was Mr. Darcy who occupied most of her thoughts, and her uncertainty about his reason for leaving was a strong inducement for her to travel. The Bingleys, she hoped, might be able to tell her more. Of course, if he had gone straight back to Cornwall, they might not be able to tell her anything.

Her strongest hope, however, was that she might be able to see him and have a chance to apologize.

∞ ∞ ∞

It was raining heavily when Elizabeth arrived at Jane's townhouse and she was forced to dig hastily for her pattens to put them on. She needed to wade through the stream of water running down the side of the street to get to the steps. While she did not mind getting mud on her dress in the country, in Town it was a completely different matter.

The townhouse where her sister lived was a modest one, not far from Uncle Gardiners' on Church Street. As she went up the stairs, the door opened, and the housekeeper gave Elizabeth a welcome smile.

"Are you keeping well, Mrs. Flynn?"

"Yes, thank you, Miss Bennet. You'd better step in from the rain. We've lit a fire in your chamber, so if you feel the need to change out of your travel clothes, the room is warm and cozy. Mrs. Munstead has been expecting you all day. She's attending to something, but I'm sure she'll be upstairs in a few minutes. I'll have tea ready for when you're done."

The kindness of Mrs. Flynn warmed her heart. She took off the pattens and knocked the mud out of them as she stepped nimbly into the house.

A maid was sent up with Elizabeth to help her dress and to unpack her portmanteau. Elizabeth had barely had time to give instructions to the maid when there was a knock on the door. It opened, and Jane's blonde head appeared.

"May I come in?"

"Of course."

Jane entered, carrying seven-month-old Lucille.

"Look at her! How much she's grown! She's a split image of her mother, make no mistake." Elizabeth put out her hands. "Here, come to me, Lucy."

The baby shrank back.

"She's a bit shy, especially with strangers."

Elizabeth realized she ought to have visited earlier. She did not like the idea that her niece didn't know her. "I'm not a stranger."

"Of course not, but she hasn't seen you for four months, and if you consider how young she is, that is a very long time."

Elizabeth nodded. "She was just a small babe when I last saw her."

"Lucy can turn over now, and she can sit up," said the proud parent. She put her daughter down on her stomach. "Show auntie Lizzy what you can do."

The child turned at once, then with a struggle, managed to pull herself up into a sitting position.

"That's amazing! When did you get so clever, Lucy?"

The child gurgled and sucked at her fists. Elizabeth couldn't resist. She went over to her, tickled her tummy, showered her chubby face with kisses, and swooped her up.

Jane watched her daughter fondly for a few minutes as Elizabeth played with her, then rang the pull bell.

"We'd better go down, Lizzy. Mrs. Flynn will have tea waiting for us. Besides, I'm dying to hear your news, and it's impossible to talk with Lucy distracting us."

The nanny appeared, and Elizabeth handed over the little girl reluctantly. Jane sat down on her sister's bed and waited.

"What news from home, Lizzy? And what brings you here so urgently? I know you said it is nothing to worry about, but it isn't like you to come to London with so little notice."

Elizabeth hesitated as she considered where to start. She had written very little to Jane about Mr. Darcy, and she wasn't sure exactly how to explain what had happened without revealing Mr. Darcy's identity.

"This is about Mr. Bingley, isn't it? Do you intend to call on the Bingleys? Because I was thinking it might be too forward under the circumstances." She took Elizabeth's hand between hers. "If he is not—that is, if he—"

Elizabeth smiled. "You may say it, Jane. If he does not care for me. I have thought it often enough, but everyone seems to avoid stating it." She looked at their entwined hands and gave Jane's a squeeze. "I *shall* call on the Bingleys, naturally. There can be no objection to calling on his sisters, Jane, surely."

"But you have no idea why Mr. Bingley left. Supposing he felt trapped and he wanted to escape making a commitment? Unless there is something you're not telling me. "

"There is nothing to tell. Everything was going along swimmingly when suddenly Mr. Bingley was up and gone. Can we talk about something else, please? Everyone in Meryton asks me the same questions, and I'm heartily sick of it."

"You need not pretend to be brave to me, Lizzy. You thought yourself on the verge of being engaged, and now nothing has come of it. You must be heartbroken."

Elizabeth tried to work out how she felt about it. "If I am heartbroken, it is not at all what they say it is. I am upset, and hurt, but most of all, I'm embarrassed. I never thought I would be the object of pity, nor of gloating, either, and our neighbors are divided between one or the other. Some console me by saying I was aiming too high, others condemn me for it."

"For aiming too high? How is that?"

"The Bingleys are very refined, well-mannered and exceptionally accomplished, much more than you and I. We didn't have the advantage of a governess or a finishing school. Moreover, Mr. Bingley is handsome, universally liked, has inherited a fortune of a hundred thousand, and has made Netherfield his country home – well, there are a great many reasons for him to be considered superior to us."

"For someone who does not particularly care for Mr. Bingley, you are certainly painting a picture of perfection."

"Do you think so? You see, I have no experience of falling in love, and perhaps I am expecting too much. I will know, I suppose, when I see him again, and if my heart does not fall to my feet or some such thing, I will know then that I am not in love."

Jane regarded her soberly. "Will you marry him, if he asks, even if you don't love him?"

"It is impossible not to love Mr. Bingley. Everyone does. But to be in love is another matter entirely. I cannot decide now. It will have to wait until -- and if -- I ever set eyes on him again."

"Perhaps you could call on the Bingleys and leave your calling card without visiting. It would then be up to them to acknowledge your acquaintance by calling on you."

"That's a good idea," said Elizabeth. She wanted to talk to the Bingleys as soon as possible but she would rather not appear on their doorstep unexpectedly. It might be very awkward if they refused to see her. Better to prepare them by letting them know she was here. "Well, then, now that we have decided on our course of action, let us talk about other matters."

Jane smiled and came to her feet. "Come downstairs and have some tea and refreshments, and you can tell me all the latest news from Meryton."

∞ ∞ ∞

The next day, they called on the Bingleys and Elizabeth left her calling card, then returned to Gracechurch street, where they took advantage of the dry weather to look into the shop windows and examine the silks and cottons that filled the warehouses.

"Why don't you pick some material you like? I thought we might have a new walking dress made for you."

Elizabeth was not so indifferent to fashion not to be tempted. However, she was aware that the pin money Mr. Bennet had given her did not extend to buying a new gown.

"I will content myself with getting a new length of muslin and some ribbons. That is as much shopping as I intend to do."

"Never mind what *you* intend, Lizzy. *I* intend to treat you to a new dress."

"Jane, you are the kindest sister in the universe, but you must not squander your pin money on me. I assure you, I have no need of a new dress."

"Don't you want to impress a certain gentleman?" Jane poked her in the ribs and gave her a meaningful smile. "You cannot win a modish gentleman's affections dressed in last year's pattern."

Elizabeth thought of Miss Bingley, with her air of fashionable elegance. It would be good to appear before her in something new, and made, moreover, by a London modiste.

"True enough. But are you quite certain it will not strain your finances? I do not want you to economize for my sake."

"Mr. Munstead may not be as rich as Mr. Bingley, but we live comfortably enough. We employ a modest number of servants and we do not entertain extravagantly, but Mr. Munstead is more than happy to pay for fripperies and gowns, as long as it is not excessive. He will be happy to see you well dressed."

Elizabeth arched her brow and laughed. "I am not so poorly dressed as all that, surely?"

Jane blushed and looked confused. "No, indeed. That was not what I meant--"

Elizabeth reached over and put her hand over Jane's. "You must know that I'm teasing you, Jane, surely."

Jane looked relieved. "Thank heavens. Yes, I do remember you like to tease. I have missed our time together. You must come to London more often, Lizzy."

"You know Papa cannot spare me. He says he does not like to be left alone in a household full of silly women."

"Papa can be cruel, sometimes."

"I think you have been away too long. Lydia and Kitty prattle on about fashion and gossip, Mary is unbearably tedious, and mama is attentive to no one but her poor nerves."

Jane choked back a giggle. "You must not talk that way, Lizzy. You know you must not."

"Very well, then. Let us go back to discussing fashion, if that is what makes you more comfortable. I would be happy to accept your offer of a new gown. You have shamed me into accepting, when clearly my own clothes will not do in your jaded London eyes. I will bow to your superior judgement."

"Now you are teasing again. Still, I am glad you have accepted. You must not be formal with me now that I'm married, Lizzy. What are sisters for, after all?"

∞ ∞ ∞

Elizabeth had been a week in town without either seeing or hearing from Caroline Bingley. If she needed any confirmation of Charlotte's explanation in her letter, she now had it. The Bingleys did not wish to pursue any connection with the Bennets. By now her anger at Mr. Darcy's intervention had diminished a great deal. After all, if Mr. Bingley had allowed himself to be so easily persuaded, then surely his attachment was too weak to be worth pursuing.

Jane accounted for it, however, by supposing that her calling card had, by some accident, been lost, or that the Bingleys were out of town.

"We will ask aunt Gardiner what she thinks. Perhaps she will have some suggestion about what to do."

Elizabeth was reluctant to pursue the matter any further. She could see no purpose in continuing an acquaintance which was obviously over.

When Elizabeth went to see her aunt, however, Mrs. Gardiner convinced her that it was worth a try to call again.

"You have nothing to lose. We will go together. If they do not admit us, then you will have final confirmation. Until then, you can't be certain."

"I don't wish to intrude where I am not wanted."

"You cannot possibly know the reason for their neglect." Her aunt smiled at her. "You are making too many assumptions based on nothing at all. It isn't like you to give up without a fight, Lizzy."

It was ironic, because she did not have anything in particular that she was fighting for. However, she did want to know about Mr. Darcy. She was willing to put up with the Bingleys' indifference if she could discover what had happened to him.

She smiled. "You are absolutely right. I cannot give in without a fight."

Mrs. Gardiner agreed to take her the next day by carriage.

"If we do not succeed in gaining admittance, we will console ourselves by going for ices at Gunter's."

The next morning, Elizabeth, Jane and Mrs. Gardiner presented themselves at Louisa Hurst's townhouse where Miss Bingley resided with her sister. Elizabeth gave her name to the butler and, to everyone's relief, they were led to the drawing room, where

Miss Bingley and Mrs. Hurst were already entertaining several of their acquaintances.

"Miss Bennet," said Miss Bingley, once all the introductions had been made. "When did you arrive in Town? You should have let me know you were coming, and I would have called on you."

The look Miss Bingley exchanged with Mrs. Hurst, however, told Elizabeth all she needed to know. They had known about her presence in London and chosen to ignore it. Elizabeth felt all the awkwardness of her situation, particularly since she could not ask about Mr. Darcy in front of strangers.

The visit went on for the requisite twenty minutes, in which everyone talked about absolutely nothing. The other visitors took their leave, but there was no opportunity for Elizabeth to question Miss Bingley about Mr. Darcy until it was time to depart.

To Elizabeth's surprise, Miss Bingley seemed to be expecting the question.

"Ah, yes, the trial. Everyone is talking about the trial. Personally, I don't understand why he handed himself in, but then I have never understood Mr. Darcy."

Elizabeth stared at her in shock. "The trial?"

Miss Bingley looked at her pityingly.

"I see you have not heard." She put her fingers to the turquoise cross she was wearing and began to move it back and forth on its chain. "Mr. Darcy is in prison. He is to be tried for murder."

Chapter 18

The shot rang out, followed by a grunt of pain. Darcy ran over to where Wickham lay on the ground and kneeled next to him.

"The apothecary is here, Wickham. He will see to you."

"Darcy. You bag of worms." The sneer on his face turned into a grimace. "You win." The words turned into a wheeze. "Always been the lucky one." He turned sideways to cough. Blood trickled from the side of his mouth. He reached out to grab Darcy's coat.

"Hope— you— suffer and burn—I will—haunt—" The rasping broke off.

Darcy stared in horror as Wickham's face turned into a skull before his very eyes. His skeletal hands, his bones stripped of flesh and blood, reached towards Darcy, making a clacking sound as they moved, the bones scraping against each other. The fingers arched around Darcy's neck, the thumb sliding into the hollow at the bottom of his throat. Darcy tried to move, but he was gripped by a numbness that prevented him. He edged his fingers under the bones, struggling to pry them free, but Wickham's skeleton was possessed of superhuman strength. Darcy writhed and kicked out. Already white stars were dancing in front of his eyes. He could no longer breathe—

Darcy bolted upright in bed. He was drenched in sweat, his pulse thundering in his ears. He took in great gulps of air to ease the tightness in his throat.

Slowly, the vividness of the nightmare began to fade, and he relaxed against the bedframe. He hadn't had a nightmare for several months now, and he was beginning to hope they had gone for good.

He didn't always dream about Wickham. Sometimes he dreamt about things he had seen on the battlefield. At times he dreamt that a bayonet was rushing towards him. Sometimes he saw fallen comrades and heard their cries of pain. He wanted to do something, anything, but was unable to save them. Sometimes Wickham was on the battlefield, and flashes of the past were all jumbled together.

Sitting in the darkness alone would not make the nightmares go away. That much he knew by now.

Darcy rose, struck the tinderbox, and lit a candle. The candlelight cast a dull light over his surroundings, and he thought he saw a rat scuttle into a corner. At least the light chased the nightmare away.

Darcy took up the claret decanter that he had started the night before and poured himself a glass, sitting backwards in a sprawl. He ran his hand along the stubble on his cheek. He was paying for a man to shave him, but the man didn't always show up. It was a constant reminder of how much he was at the mercy of his jailor, and how dependent he was on being able to grease someone's palm.

Yet he could hardly complain. Prison was not intended for convenience, and he was far better off than the poor souls who did not have the money to make their stay comfortable. The fire burned merrily and kept him warm inside the damp stone walls, the pile of firewood in the corner was always refurbished, he had good claret to drink and a comfortable feather mattress to sleep on. For Darcy, that was luxury enough. During his time at the battlefront, he had become hardened to living without certain luxuries, although of course officers – even humble ones like Darcy – did far better than the common soldier.

His mind shied away from memories of the battlefield. Absently, he rubbed his thumb against the scar on his knee. Scars were best forgotten. He did his best not to relive the screams and the smells. He could not help but feel it was ironic that he was imprisoned for the death of one man, when on the battlefield it had been perfectly acceptable to kill so many.

Of course, there was a difference. Killing in defense of King and Country was very different from killing a man in cold blood, but there were moments when Wickham's death blended in with that of others. Wickham's eyes became the eyes of another man in battle – reflecting the instant the man realized that death was upon him, the knowledge that all was over, the fading of light. Sometimes it was hard to tell them apart.

Damn you, Darcy, damn you to all eternity. Those had been Wickham's dying words, and they haunted him daily. At times Darcy wondered whether a noose around his neck would not be preferable to living with his guilt.

Except that he refused to die for the sake of a despicable man like Wickham. He would never forget the instant that he had arrived in Margate, only to discover that Wickham had convinced his sister to elope to Gretna Green with him. He had caught up with them when they stopped at a wayside inn. Not a moment too soon.

He could never regret challenging a man who would have deflowered a fifteen-year-old girl and robbed her of both her innocence and inheritance without the smallest shred of remorse. If Wickham had succeeded in his machinations, he would have destroyed Georgiana's life completely. What kind of a future would Georgiana have had, once Wickham had taken her money and abandoned her for his usual debauchery and gambling? Already tainted in the eye of society for running off with Wickham, she would have been the object of pity, gossip and censure. Wickham's misdeeds would follow her wherever she was, fueling the air of scandal surrounding her for the rest of her life – or at least until Wickham drank himself into an early death.

No, Darcy did not have any choice but to challenge Wickham to a duel. He had not intended to kill Wickham, only to teach him a lesson

However, he would not allow Wickham to be the victor. It was enough that Darcy was cursed with the knowledge that he had killed his childhood companion. He would live with the guilt all his life. However, he intended to do whatever he could to stay alive.

His thoughts went to Miss Elizabeth Bennet. She, too, haunted him and filled him with guilt, though in a very different way. He could still hear the ring of her accusations in his ear. He had not meant to hurt her, yet he had, and then he had left without even letting her know why. He should have told her he was leaving. What would she think of him now? Would she discover the truth? How long before word reached Meryton and everyone knew of his fall from grace?

$$\infty \quad \infty \quad \infty$$

The horror of Miss Bingley's pronouncement struck Elizabeth to the core. Worse, she had the feeling that Miss Bingley was enjoying the opportunity to pass on the gossip, even if it was at the expense of Mr. Darcy.

"How can you say such a thing about a friend of your brother's?"

"I assure you, I am not the one saying these things. The whole of London is following the trial with interest."

Miss Bingley took up a copy of *The Times* from the table and handed it to her. A small column was circled.

Having surrendered to the magistrate at Bow Street, Fitzwilliam Darcy is to stand trial on March 20 at Old Bailey for manslaughter following the death of George Wickham after a duel.

Elizabeth felt a surge of relief that Mr. Darcy was guilty of a crime of honor at least. It did not lesson her anxiety for him, but it made him less of a guilty party in her eyes. She put down the newspaper.

"Thank you for informing me of the situation, Miss Bingley. Meanwhile, I hope you will convey my regards to your brother."

The ladies took their leaves. Elizabeth remained tight lipped until the footman had closed the door of the carriage and removed the step. There she threw herself back against the squabs and wrung her hands in agitation.

"Did you see how indifferent she was to Mr. Darcy's predicament? she said. "How could she be so heartless when his fate lies in the balance?"

"It is indeed very shocking," said Jane.

"Surely the fact that he turned himself in should count to his advantage." Elizabeth was in the grip of anxiety.

"He is not the first gentleman to fight a duel," said Mrs. Gardiner. "I am sure he would not have done so without provocation."

"But what if they find him guilty?"

An ominous silence descended upon the carriage as everyone thought of what that verdict would mean.

∞ ∞ ∞

The prospect of waiting docilely for three weeks until the trial was too dreadful for Elizabeth to contemplate. She needed to see Mr. Darcy and talk to him. She could not bear the idea that she had added to Mr. Darcy's misery because of her accusations. It was quite possible that, in the scheme of things, her attack on him was not very important, but she felt she owed him an apology. She could only imagine the suffering he must be going through at being the object of speculation and finger pointing. If friends like the Bingleys had abandoned him, she wanted him to know that not everyone had.

It was very clear, however, that she could not just simply decide to visit Mr. Darcy in jail. That would imply too much of an intimacy between them, and besides, she had no idea how to go about bribing the authorities to admit her.

After a great deal of thought, she arrived at a way of doing so without arousing too many questions. She would ask Jane's husband for his assistance. She could kill two birds with one stone. If Mr. Munstead would agree to help in Mr. Darcy's defense, she could both be in a position to do something useful, as well as having an opportunity to visit Mr. Darcy and show her support. She considered that either of those things may well mean nothing to Mr. Darcy himself, who would very likely have a superior legal counsel, and who would be too preoccupied with his own problems to care whether she had forgotten their quarrel. She did it for herself, and she would feel better, she knew, if she did not stand on the sidelines and watch.

Having made up her mind, Elizabeth lost no time that evening explaining Mr. Darcy's situation to Mr. Munstead, who already had some inkling of the case from what he had read in the news sheets.

"I am not certain what you want me to do, Miss Bennet. I have no doubt Mr. Darcy will have excellent advice. Lawyers, as you know, are not usually admitted to trials, and if Mr. Darcy has hired one, that will be more than enough."

"Yes, but they say two heads are better than one, and there may be something Mr. Darcy's legal counsel may have missed. Think of it as a favor to your sister."

Mr. Munstead gave her a searching glance.

"You are concerning yourself very closely with this gentleman's affairs."

The statement brought a flush to her face.

"He is a good friend. I would not want him to come to any harm. I wish to do anything I can to help him."

"Very well, but I hope you will not be offended if I warn you that you shouldn't be associating with a person embroiled in scandal. A young lady cannot be too careful, you know."

Elizabeth chewed at her lower lip. "I'm well aware of that, sir. I only intend to accompany you this first time."

Mr. Munstead was taken aback, and immediately objected to her visiting the prisoner at all.

"There is no need at all for you to be there at all, Miss Bennet."

"Perhaps there is no need, but I would like to show Mr. Darcy my support."

Mr. Munstead shook his head and looked towards Jane.

"I hope you will convince your sister, Jane, that this visit could do more harm than good."

Jane smiled and shook her head. "I have never been able to talk Lizzy out of anything, once she has set her mind on it. You may have more success than I will."

Mr. Munstead reiterated what he had said earlier and tried again at dinner to dissuade her. She listened to his argument politely. However, nothing he said could convince her otherwise, and in the end, Mr. Munstead was resigned to taking her with him, providing she promised to wear a veil, and not reveal her identity.

∞ ∞ ∞

The next day, the turnkey opened the door at an unexpected hour and announced that Darcy had a visitor. A moment later, Bingley put his head through the door and grinned.

Seeing Bingley brought a rush of guilt. He had been thinking of Miss Bennet and what she had said to him – about how he had manipulated his closest friend into abandoning the woman he loved. What was it about him that made Darcy hurt the people closest to him, the very ones– yes, he would admit it to himself – he loved most in the world? He had hurt Georgiana, Bingley, and then Miss Bennet. He had dragged the family name through the mud. He was apparently intent on destroying everything he had ever cared for.

"You should not be here, Bingley. Better leave me to my own devices." His voice was harsh.

"Don't be absurd, Darcy. What kind of a friend would I be if I did that?"

A better friend than Darcy was, he thought. He had torn Bingley away from the woman he loved for his own selfish reasons. Darcy wanted her for himself. He had not known it at the time, which was some excuse, he supposed, but the shameful truth was there for anyone to see.

What was it Bingley had asked him? Ah, yes.

"A sensible friend," said Darcy.

"But that's just it, Darcy. I'm not at all sensible. You know I do everything on impulse."

"Then for once, Bingley, curb your impulse. Wait until I'm out of here. Don't ruin your future by associating with me."

If he ever got out of here.

Bingley ignored him, and looked around at the damp room, taking in the mildew on the windows and the dirty floor.

"Are they treating you right? I have just paid the warden handsomely to allow my servant to deliver food to you. He will eat some of it, no doubt, but that's a good incentive, I suppose."

Darcy was touched. "I appreciate it, Bingley. However, I still advise you to stay away, if not for your sake, for your sister's. I hope she is well, by the way."

Bingley did not meet his eye. "She is well. She left town today, to spend some time at a friend's house party."

Darcy surmised from Bingley's remark that Miss Bingley, at least, was being sensible and keeping as far away from him as possible. He could not blame her – in fact, that was precisely what he would have advocated – but it still rankled. Darcy was sure she had also advised her brother to stay away from Darcy.

"You would do well to heed her advice."

The guilty flush on Bingley's face confirmed his surmise. "I will not abandon a friend," said Bingley, "especially not a friend in need." They shared some claret and talked about trivial things. Bingley told him about the house party he had attended, but Darcy was too distracted to talk of dancing and hunting, and his mind kept wondering to Miss Bennet. Should he say anything to Bingley about her? He could not make up his mind. He was torn and could not come to a decision.

Bingley, no doubt feeling Darcy's distraction, soon got up to leave, promising to visit again soon, and Darcy was relieved that the decision had been postponed.

Nevertheless, Darcy felt Bingley's absence keenly the moment he left. It was very lonely in jail. He was accustomed to solitude, but this was of a very different kind. Being confined to a small space made all the difference. Not knowing how and when it all may end made everything seem worse.

His thoughts, as always, turned to Miss Bennet with longing. Would he ever have a chance to see her again, he wondered? It was too painful to consider he might not.

∞ ∞ ∞

A few hours later, to Darcy's astonishment, the door was unlocked again, and it creaked open.

"A visitor for you, Mr. Darcy. A young lady and a gentleman."

The turnkey stepped aside to allow a tall young lady, her face covered by a gauze veil, into the room. Then a gentleman came in behind her. It was his cousin Richard. As the jailor left and locked the door, the lady put up the gauze veil from her face.

"Georgiana!"

Darcy stood up quickly. She flew at him, knocking him backwards. His arms came out to hold her. She was sobbing.

"Oh, William, I have missed you so much!"

A lump rose to his throat. He was in danger of sobbing himself, confound it. Only an iron will and the knowledge that he ought to be stronger than his little sister held him in check.

"Let me look at you," he said, tearing her from his shoulder and holding her at arm's length. "You know, I don't have a maid here to launder my clothes, so if you soil them with your tears, I will have to endure it for many days to come."

That made Georgiana laugh, as he had hoped. She had grown since the last time he'd seen her, not so much in height but in her appearance. She had shed her childhood and become a young woman. There were circles under her eyes and an edginess to her face. She had suffered. They had both suffered, and all because of that scoundrel. Anger surfaced again, an anger he thought he had put behind him a long time ago.

He didn't want his sister to see it, so he gave Georgiana's hands a quick squeeze then turned to Richard.

"I see you've been looking after my sister well, Cousin!" He put out his hand and clasped Fitzwilliam's arm strongly.

His cousin smiled. "Of course I have. Did you doubt it? I am glad you have had a chance to see her, finally. You should have turned yourself in some time ago and saved us all a lot of anxiety."

And drag Georgiana's name through the mud? Never! "You know why I couldn't do that. Even now I will try everything to prevent a scandal." He was trying not to refer to Georgiana, but she understood him at once.

"All this is my fault. My own stupidity! I have ruined three years of your life."

He shook his head. "On the contrary. If it were not for this, I would never have had an opportunity to go abroad, see something of the world, to experience what others experience. I have been to Spain, to Portugal, and to France. I have slept in the outdoors under the stars and marched through mountains. If it were not for this, I would have gone on as I always did, tending to the estate at Pemberley and never changing." He had meant to reassure her, but as he said the words, he was surprised to discover that he meant them. They were entirely true. He was a different person now. He had grown and developed.

He would not have had the opportunity to meet Miss Bennet and fall in love.

"So you need not blame yourself, you see. You gave me the chance to do something different." He smiled at her.

Her eyes glistened with tears.

"You have always been too good to me, Brother."

Had he? He wondered. He had often wondered in the past three years if it had not been his fault that Wickham had managed to gain access to Georgiana, for many reasons. If he had been there for his sister, would Wickham have been able to take advantage of her loneliness?

"In any case, the past is not what matters. It's the present that counts. We will have to manage the whole thing very carefully. We do not want to destroy any chance you may have of marriage by allowing anyone to think you were compromised. I appreciate that you came to see me, Georgiana, but I would prefer you to be very far from here, in case of any unpleasantness."

Fitzwilliam cleared his throat. "As for that – well, that's why Georgiana and I are here – or at least, one of the reasons. We wanted to talk to you." He looked at Georgiana. She nodded encouragingly. The strained look on her face had disappeared and there was a glow to her face and a special light in her eyes.

What was this? A new development? Since when did Fitzwilliam look to Georgiana for permission to speak?

"I have come to ask your permission to marry Georgiana."

Darcy looked from one to the other. Richard was looking tenderly at his sister, and Georgiana's face was luminous.

So that was where the wind blew, then. His sense of relief was intense. If Georgiana was married to the one man who knew exactly what had happened that fateful evening, the scandal would not hurt her chances. It would not be easy, but with her husband by her side to help her weather the storm, it would make it all so much easier.

However, it was all entirely too convenient. The timing was very suspicious. He could understand Fitzwilliam's motivation. Georgiana was an heiress, and his cousin was a younger son with no prospects.

And he knew Georgiana all too well. Given the circumstances, Georgiana was all too likely to be willing to sacrifice herself for her brother. She would do anything to free Darcy from feeling responsible.

He looked from one to the other, trying to gauge the situation.

"May I speak to Georgiana privately, Fitzwilliam?"

"Certainly." Fitzwilliam went to the door and knocked to be let out.

As soon as the door shut once again, Darcy turned to his sister. He examined her gravely, trying to understand how she was feeling.

"If you are doing this simply because you think it will ease my conscience, little sister, I hope you will reconsider. I do not want you giving up the chance to marry someone of your own choice. Richard is a good man, but he is much older than you. Patience, Georgiana. If you wait a while, you will be able to come to London again when everything is blown over. It is not impossible for you to find a husband, in spite of everything."

Georgiana let out a cry of protest. "No, no! You have it all wrong. It is not like that at all!"

"How is it, then? Do you deny that you are doing this out of duty? I did not save you from Wickham to have you fall prey to another fortune hunter."

She gasped. "Fortune hunter? Are you referring to Richard?"

"Surely you know by now that your fortune is a big temptation?"

Darcy looked at her severely.

She twisted her hands together and looked to the ground. "No, you are wrong about this, William."

She looked up, then, and met Darcy's gaze. She was angry.

"No, William. You should know better than to think Fitzwilliam a fortune hunter! After all our cousin has done for you! He has done the impossible to learn to manage the estate. He is the kindest, most caring—" Her voice trembled. "—how can you possibly compare him to someone like Wickham!"

Her passionate defense of his cousin went a long way towards convincing him that Georgiana cared for Richard, but he wanted her to be absolutely certain.

"Very well, Fitzwilliam may not be a fortune hunter, but how can you think of marrying someone who is so many years your senior? Again, are you certain you are not marrying him out of gratitude, because he was there when I was not?"

He held his breath. This was important for him, because he knew he had been forced to abandon Georgiana.

Georgiana held up her chin. "It is true that I do feel a sense of gratitude to him, but not because I feel that you were not there for me. To be honest, I spent much of my childhood alone while you were away. I missed you a great deal, but your letters were frequent and I never felt you had left me. This has been little different."

He had not known how much tension he was holding. He released it after hearing her words. She did not resent him, then, either for what he had done to Wickham, or for staying away afterwards.

"You have not yet answered me, Georgiana," he probed, more gently now. "Are you doing this because you are under a sense of obligation to him?"

She shook her head. "No," she said firmly. "We spent a great deal of time together, you know. He was at Pemberley all the time. I have come to – love him." She blushed.

The blush told him all he needed to know.

"But will he make you happy?"

Her eyes glimmered. "I am happier now than I have ever been. I believe I have found – my soul mate." The last words were little more than a whisper. Her face had turned bright red.

Darcy could not help it. He laughed. A huge burden had tumbled off his back and he felt giddy with relief. "Then I could not be happier for you, little sister."

He moved towards her and kissed her on her brow. "I wish you every happiness, Georgiana."

"Then I have your blessing?" Her eyes held tears.

He nodded. "Absolutely. You have every blessing I could possibly bestow on you."

∞ ∞ ∞

At last Darcy had something cheerful to think about. Even if something were to happen to him – well, he knew Georgiana's future, as well as the future of Pemberley – was secure. All had turned out well. He could face his own future, whatever it held, without fearing that anyone would suffer.

The sense of relief and gladness had not fully dissipated the next day when, yet again, a visitor was announced.

"This is the last time, mind," warned the jailor, muttering and shaking his head. "If I had known you'd be holding a bloody reception I would have put a limit on how many people could visit. A Miss Smith to see you, sir, and a Mr. Munstead."

Darcy could not imagine who the visitors could be. He frowned, waiting to find out who they were. A young lady with a veil on her face hovered in the doorway, accompanied by a gentleman he had never met.

"Go in, go in," said the jailor, impatiently, all but pushing them into the room and slamming the door behind them.

The figure of the lady before him was so familiar that for a moment he thought he was imagining it. His heart lurched violently. Surely his mind was playing tricks on him.

But then she moved forward, and he caught a whiff of her scent.

He leapt to his feet. It was Elizabeth. It was impossible, but it was truly her.

∞ ∞ ∞

When they first entered, Mr. Darcy was seated at a table, reading. He stood up as they came in. As his gaze fell on her, there was something almost wild to it. Its intensity confused her. Why was he looking at her like that? Was her visit really that improper? She felt torn by several impulses. She wanted to run to Mr. Darcy and throw her arms around him, but she also felt she should leave. It was a mistake to have come, to have intruded on him this way. Well, she was here, and she could hardly turn and flee.

Somehow, she managed to hold herself together as she realized belatedly that she had not even greeted him.

She gave a little bob. "I hope you are well, Mr. Darcy?" She was relieved that her voice was steady, even if it was tighter than usual.

Meanwhile, Mr. Darcy was beginning to look more like himself.

He bowed. "I am as well as expected. Miss—Smith. I did not expect to see you – in London."

"No."

"Are you staying long?"

"I am not quite certain how long."

He nodded. "Your parents are in good health?"

"Yes. Very well, thank you."

"And your sisters?"

"Yes, very well."

"When did you arrive in Town?"

"I arrived yesterday. I am staying at my sisters' house on Church Street."

"Yes, of course."

Mr. Munstead cleared his throat.

Elizabeth turned to introduce her brother. "I have brought my brother-in-law, Mr. Munstead. Mr. Darcy, this is Mr. Munstead. He is an attorney, and by all accounts a good one. I thought you might be able to consult with him on legal matters. He had a few ideas about the defense. Even if you have your own legal counsel, he may be able to help."

Please don't turn me down, she thought. *Please let me do something for you.*

∞ ∞ ∞

She had done this for him! She had come to see him, and she had brought someone to help. She did not hate him for what he had done to her, and she did not condemn him for what he had done. He did not know what to say. He was overwhelmed by her kindness. He did not deserve it.

He needed to say something. "Mr. Munstead. I would very much appreciate your advice. My cousin Richard will be collecting character witnesses, and we have a defense counsel set up, but I would welcome all the suggestions I can get."

"Then if you don't mind, I'd like to ask you some questions."

"Of course."

Darcy hoped he had a great many questions. He had wanted to tell Miss Bennet the truth about his past. This was his chance. He would tell his story, and now there would no longer be any secrets between them.

Chapter 19

The day of the trial, in the early morning, Mr. Darcy wrote several letters. It was unnecessary to do it now, but he was not sure what state of mind he would be in if the court hearing did not go his way. He would feel better if he could write to everyone when his mind was clear.

The first of his letters was addressed to Bingley. It was time to clear his conscience and to give Miss Bennet the chance to be happy as she deserved.

Dear Bingley,

Miss Bennet is a priceless jewel, and even with the disadvantage of her relations, you will do well together. Having thought about it carefully, I think I may have overestimated the influence her family will have on your life. If the two of you care for each other, as I believe you do, I think you owe it to her to ask for her hand in marriage.

In other words, my dear fellow, I give my blessings – not that you are in need of them – and wish you every happiness in the future.

Sincerely,

Your friend, Darcy

The other letters were addressed to Georgiana, Richard, and other of his relations. The last one he hesitated over a great deal, but decided he would only have it delivered if the verdict went very badly indeed. It was addressed to Miss Elizabeth Bennet.

As he wrote it, he trembled with the effort of trying not to tell her his own feelings. He could not. The letter was an apology to her for causing her so much unhappiness, and it offered his congratulations on her future marriage with Bingley. By the end, he felt utterly drained by the effort of writing. It was the most difficult task he had ever completed. He sat thinking about it, about how things could have been different.

It was almost a relief when Richard arrived to accompany him to the Old Bailey, where the jury awaited him.

One way or the other, his fate would soon be sealed.

∞ ∞ ∞

The trial lasted twenty minutes, in which the jury heard several character testimonies. Hollins had appeared to testify for the prosecution, but his testimony was discredited by another witness who asserted he had been too drunk to remember what had happened.

Based on the testimony of the surgeon, and of the seconds of both parties, and of several of his friends who offered character references, the conclusion of the jury was that Mr. Darcy had justifiable reason to demand a duel, and that there had been no intent to commit murder. Mr. Wickham had shot first and had wounded Mr. Darcy in the shoulder. Mr. Darcy had merely intended to teach Mr. Wickham a lesson by wounding him in the arm, and had stated the same to his seconds, but Mr. Wickham was drunk, and had stumbled at the last minute. The bullet had struck Mr. Wickham in the lungs, with the consequence that Mr. Wickham had not survived the wound.

Moreover, the fact that Mr. Darcy had remained at Mr. Wickham's side all through the night, even after he died, was another point in his favor. It was clear that he had suffered upon Wickham's demise, which further proved that he had no malicious intent of murdering the deceased.

A few minutes later, after a short deliberation, the jury passed their verdict. Mr. Darcy was acquitted, and it was all over.

Darcy could scarcely believe that the matter had been resolved so quickly. He stood in court, trying to accustom himself to the idea, and had to be ushered out as the next defendant was brought in.

Still too numb to appreciate his good fortune, Darcy returned to the prison to collect his letters. He stared at the one addressed to Miss Bennet for several moments, then lit a candle and burned it. With a firm step, he strode towards the door, and gave the turnkey several coins as he went through. He crossed the damp hallway with long easy strides. The guards opened the door and let him out. He stood looking onto the street. It seemed hardly possible he did not have to look over his shoulder anymore to see if anyone recognized him. He was free to do whatever he chose, to go wherever he chose.

As he waited for Richard to bring round the carriage to pick him up, he finally understood that the nightmare was over, and that he was free, and began to think about what he wanted to do next.

His heart whispered: Netherfield. He contemplated that possibility, indulging in a fantasy of returning there. He would make his way across to Longbourn as soon as he arrived and invite Miss Bennet to walk with him on Oakham Mount. He would tell her how much he loved her and would invite her to be his wife.

He quashed the fantasy quickly. She belonged to someone else. There was no chance at all that such a thing could ever happen.

∞ ∞ ∞

Having received everyone's congratulations, Darcy's first port of call was Mr. Munstead's house. He owed Miss Bennet the courtesy of thanking her for her assistance, and of informing her of the verdict, though no doubt she had already heard it from Mr. Munstead.

As he was ushered into the drawing room, the sight of Elizabeth – so enchanting, yet so out of his reach – reduced him to silence. He supposed he managed to bow to Mrs. Munstead, and utter some polite greeting, but his whole being was centered on Miss Bennet. He strode across the room to where she was standing, took up her hand and brushed his lips lightly across it. He did not stroke her palm with his thumb as he longed to do, but he felt the soft flutter of her fingers like a caress. It was agony being so close and not being able to draw her to him, but he stood his ground, drawing on all his reserves as a gentleman. His gaze wandered over her face, feasting on her, wanting to memorize her features before he let her go. Her image would haunt him for the rest of his life. He had an aching need to make sure he could recall every detail, from the dark swirl of her eyelashes to the rosy swell of her lips.

She was smiling, her eyebrow arched, in her usual manner.

He would gaze on her while he still could. For now, for a moment, he could pretend she was his.

He would see her again, of course, but she would be someone else's wife – as untouchable and unreachable as if she had crossed the ocean to the New World.

Her hand pulled out of his, leaving him holding nothing but air.

"Mr. Darcy." She curtseyed deeply. "I'm delighted to see you are finally free from suspicion."

"Yes," he said, trying to summon up the joy she seemed to expect. "Yes, I am free."

He didn't feel free, not at all, if anything, he felt even more shackled, as if his physical manacles had been replaced by mental ones.

She sat down on the armchair, an arm's length away from him. Having her near him but out of his reach was exquisite torment.

"Congratulations, sir."

"Thank you." He recalled the presence of Mrs. Munstead. "The efforts of Mr. Munstead were invaluable. I have just been to his office to speak to him. You must thank him again when he returns home, Mrs. Munstead. I owe a great deal to him – and to Miss Bennet."

He had so much he wanted to say to Miss Bennet, but he could not drag her into the eddying whirlpool of his life.

If she gave him just one sign, just one indication, he was prepared to fight for her, to sacrifice his friendship with Bingley for her sake. If only she showed she cared for him.

But Miss Bennet was laughing, her eyes as always alight with mischief. It was impossible not to be swept away by her laughter, even if he was feeling at breaking point.

"I'm glad my brother could be of assistance, Mr. Darcy, but I do not believe you have anything to thank me for. Mr. Munstead tells me you had plenty of character witnesses to argue your case most eloquently. I wish I could have been there."

"You need not have been there, Miss Bennet. It is the thought that counts, and I know that I had your moral support." If nothing else. He waited for her to say something, to give him the sign he was waiting for.

"That is very gallant of you, sir, but I do believe my role was very limited. I do wish I could have done more, but I see you have come out of it very well without my help. Will you and Mr. Bingley be returning to Netherfield again, then, Mr. Darcy?"

The laughter died inside him. That, there was the sign he had been waiting for, he thought bitterly. Her only concern was Mr. Bingley. As always, Bingley was the object of her interest. She cared nothing for him. Nothing at all.

Why should she? No one would want to marry a man whose name had been sullied and dragged through the mud. He should feel triumphant that he had been released and that he was a free man, but he felt hollow inside. What would he do with his freedom? There was nothing waiting for him, and, apart from Richard and Georgiana, no one who rejoiced at his discharge.

There was nothing for him here, especially. He had better be on his way. He wanted to go somewhere as far away as possible. Perhaps after Georgiana's wedding, he would go to Cornwall for a while. First, of course, he would go to Pemberley. He had been away too long.

"I will not be returning to Netherfield. I have neglected my own estate, and my sister Georgiana is to be married." He took a deep breath. It hurt him to say this, but he had to. "I am certain that if you call on the Bingleys before you leave, you will be warmly welcomed."

He did not want to see the happiness on her face, so he did not look in her direction. He came to his feet. He should have bowed and stepped away from her, once she stood up as well, but he needed one last moment, one final touch before he left her life forever.

He took up her hand. It was warm and soft and so dear to him, he longed to grasp it and bury his lips in her palm. He was seized with such a desperate desire to do that, he began to shake. In the end, he couldn't resist. He touched his lips briefly to her knuckles and felt the contact echo through his whole body.

It was agony to let go. It was like tearing part of his own skin away. The pain was too much. Unable to stay a moment longer, he dropped her hand and stepped away.

"I must leave now," he murmured. "God bless you."

He stumbled out of the room, his throat tight with bitterness and despair.

What good was freedom, when he did not have Elizabeth? At least when he had been imprisoned, he had been hopeful. Now there was no hope at all. He should have been celebrating. Instead, he was mourning what could have been.

His whole life stretched before him. He was grateful for it, because he could have been swinging at the end of a rope. He had been given another chance at living, but it was an empty life, with little chance of happiness.

He settled his hat on his head with determination. Well, if that was how it was going to be, he might as well get accustomed to it. He had survived the last three years. He would survive many more.

∞ ∞ ∞

Elizabeth stood in numb shock as Mr. Darcy walked away from her. She could not shake off the sense that there had been a note of finality to his visit and that she would not see him again. She wanted to run after him and stop him, to demand what he meant, but as the front door closed, she knew it was too late.

"How very odd! He is very abrupt, is he not?" Jane's brow was wrinkled in confusion.

Not for the first time, Elizabeth felt betrayed by Mr. Darcy. She had come to London to help and support him, then, the moment he was free, he had dismissed her entirely. Why had he come to call on her, if he was to be so cold and indifferent?

The answer was clear. He had come out of a sense of duty, to say thank you, and take his leave. Now that he was once again Master of Pemberley, the Bennets were too far beneath his notice. He was returning to his old life, and he needed to shed his inconvenient acquaintances. That was all Elizabeth was to him—an embarrassing acquaintance far beneath his notice. He had made that all too clear.

"He is arrogant and odious. Mama was right. I don't know why I wanted to help him. He thinks because his is master of Pemberley, he can run roughshod over everyone."

"To be fair, he did thank you," said Jane. "Still, I grant you, his conduct leaves a lot to be desired. He *did* leave very suddenly."

She would not cry, Elizabeth decided. She only had herself to blame, after all. What a fool she had been to think of him as a friend! Her mind went back to that first day at the Meryton Assembly when he had snubbed her. *That* was the real Mr. Darcy, deprived of all mystery. An earl's nephew could hardly be expected to treat her as an equal. She had liked plain Mr. John Darcy much better. And to think she had wanted to discover the mystery behind the man! Ha! She was an utter fool.

What had she expected when he was announced? Her heart had sung with joy that he was free – and that he had come to celebrate his freedom with her. She had not expected this cold indifference. She had thought—.

She forced herself to admit to the embarrassing hope she had harbored. How could her thoughts and feelings have leapt so quickly from friendship to matrimony?

Had she really hoped that Mr. Darcy would go on his knee right then and there and propose to her? He had stopped Mr. Bingley from marrying her because he thought she was not good enough for his friend, whose social status was not equal to Mr. Darcy of Pemberley. I am a gentleman's daughter, she wanted to say to him. How dare you think yourself superior to me?

How could she have harbored such ridiculous expectations? If he had proposed, would she have accepted him?

She knew the answer. The answer was, yes. It had been staring at her all this time, and she had not seen it. She was in love with Mr. Darcy. Of all the stupid things she could have done, this one topped it all.

"Lizzy? Are you well? You look pale. Maybe you should sit down."

Elizabeth shook her head at her sister, and, unable to utter a single word, hurried out of the room to the refuge of her bedchamber.

∞ ∞ ∞

Freedom was a strange concept, thought Darcy. He had wanted to walk free, to feel free to embrace his own identity without being haunted by the past. Yet when he went to his club, all anyone wished to talk about was his acquittal. The knocker was never still at his townhouse. Well-wishers jostled with those who came out of curiosity. Many came just in order to boast they were acquainted with an infamous man.

He had never been one to speak to strangers easily, and now, after the loneliness of the prison, being the center of attention chaffed at him. He felt confined, but he seemed incapable of making the decision to leave. He told himself he didn't want to go to Rosings before Georgiana and Richard arrived because he didn't want his aunt nagging him to marry Anne. It was too far to travel to Cornwall and back before the wedding. He thought about going to Pemberley. He missed the old place so much. But he could not simply march in and take over, as if the last three years had not existed. Richard was the master now, and although eventually he would be handing Pemberley back again, Darcy could not be so insensitive as to do it without a transition period. Besides, witnessing Georgiana and Richard's newfound happiness would only enhance his own misery and remind him of his own failure to secure the woman he loved.

Nevertheless, he knew all too well that he should not stay in London. *She* was in London, and the temptation to see her again would be too great. He had to go.

If the price of getting away was being forced to marry Anne, well, so be it. It didn't matter to him whom he married. One woman was the same as another, if it was not Elizabeth Bennet. It might as well be Anne. At least with her, he knew what to expect.

∞ ∞ ∞

Elizabeth did not call on the Bingleys. Her emotions were too turbulent to do it. If they were planning to return to Netherfield soon, there would be time enough to see them. Meanwhile, she wanted to postpone the encounter as much as possible.

If anything, she wanted to avoid them. Accordingly, she decided to delay her return home for a while. She knew that the moment she stepped through the door at Longbourn, all talk would be about Mr. Bingley's return and Mr. Darcy's disgrace. She did not want to hear anything about either gentleman. Yet she could not stay in London. There were too many bitter memories here now.

So Elizabeth wrote to her friend Charlotte Collins and hinted that, if she would be welcome, she would like to visit for two or three weeks before going home. Charlotte wrote back immediately, expressing her delight at the idea, and a date was set for Elizabeth's arrival.

∞ ∞ ∞

Three days before she was due to leave Town, Elizabeth was sitting in the parlor with her sister, when Mr. Bingley and his sister Caroline were announced. Elizabeth was surprised. She had supposed that the Bingleys had already left. The thought of being face to face with Mr. Bingley again threw her into uncertainty, but in the few seconds it took for the Bingleys to enter, she managed to compose herself.

If he asked her to marry him, she decided, in a made moment of clarity, she would say yes. There was no point in putting off the inevitable, and it was not as if marrying Mr. Bingley would be a terrible ordeal. It would work out in the end, she was sure.

As he entered, she thought, not for the first time, that he was a very handsome gentleman, and thought how lucky she was that he had singled her out.

"Miss Bennet." Miss Bingley curtseyed politely. Her manner was polite but distant. Elizabeth sensed that she was displeased, though she was doing her best to conceal it.

Could Elizabeth ever call Miss Bingley her sister? Would they ever warm to each other? She thought it unlikely.

"Miss Bingley. Mr. Bingley."

Mr. Bingley bowed deeply and professed himself to be delighted to see Elizabeth.

"It has been an age, has it not?" He gave his usual lopsided smile.

"It has," she replied, politely. "This is my sister, Mrs. Jane Munstead."

Mr. Bingley's gaze went to her sister's face. "Enchanted to meet you, Mrs. Munstead," he murmured, his face flushed.

They stood around in awkward silence. Jane invited them to sit down, but Mr. Bingley stood there, looking ill at ease.

"If you don't mind, Mrs. Munstead, I have come to talk to Miss Bennet privately, if I may."

Now that the moment was upon her, Elizabeth felt a surge of panic. Was she really going to do this? She made a beseeching gesture to Jane, who ignored it, put down her knitting, stood up, and addressed herself to Miss Bingley.

"Miss Bingley, I have heard from Elizabeth that you play the pianoforte very elegantly. I wonder if I might trouble you to look over a piece of music that I have just bought. Perhaps you can help me work out some of the more troublesome pieces."

Miss Bingley rose obliging and followed Jane out of the room, deliberately leaving the door open.

"Would you care to sit down, Mr. Bingley?" She sat down herself, but he stood in place, watching Jane and his sister as they left.

Mr. Bingley, looking red-faced and ill at ease, cleared his throat.

"Miss Bennet, you will no doubt have guessed the purpose of my visit, I hope. As you may have noticed at Netherfield, from the moment I set eyes on you, I thought you were the most beautiful woman I have met."

The words left Elizabeth completely unmoved. She willed herself to appreciate the fact that he thought her beautiful, but she could not.

"I was hoping to propose to you last November, but circumstances intervened, and I have had no chance to see you before now. I did not even know you were in town."

"It is hardly surprising, when Mr. Darcy was going through such an unpleasant experience."

"Yes, of course."

For a moment, Mr. Bingley seemed to have lost his thread.

"In any case – what I am trying to say – what I came here to do— ." He went down on one knee. "Miss Bennet, I wanted to tell you how much I admire you—"

It was all wrong. Even as Mr. Bingley was proposing, she was thinking of his friend, and how much she wished Mr. Darcy was there before her instead of Mr. Bingley. She could not bear it any longer. She could not possibly continue with this.

"Pray, Mr. Bingley, I would rather you did not continue."

Bingley flushed a dark shade of red and looked at her in astonishment.

"I don't understand, Miss Bennet."

Elizabeth looked away – out of the window at the houses opposite, at the wall, at the fireplace, anywhere rather than meet Mr. Bingley's gaze.

"I am very sorry if I gave the wrong impression when I was in Meryton, Mr. Bingley. I fear I may have misled you."

"How so?" If she wasn't in such dire straits herself, she could almost have pitied him. He looked entirely bewildered and flabbergasted.

"The fact is, if you are asking me to marry you, I cannot accept, not at this particular moment."

"Can't accept?" Bingley gaped at her as if she was mad. Perhaps he was right. Perhaps she *had* lost her mind. What on earth was she doing? She was destroying her future. She thought of mama and how terribly disappointed she was going to be. She willed herself to say yes, but the words just would not come out.

Perhaps the madness would go away. Maybe she ought be sensible and wait a while to see how she felt about this in a few months. She could not marry Mr. Bingley when she was in love with his friend. It would be an untenable situation. However, given time, when she had put her feelings for Mr. Darcy behind her, she might be able to do it.

"I cannot say yes, not at present. You must give me time. I am in an awkward situation right now, and I feel that I could not give you the answer you seek. In a few months, my answer may be different. There have been – personal circumstances that occurred while you were away. I hope you will be patient with me and give me time to consider."

Elizabeth thought she could see relief on his face, but it passed so quickly she couldn't be sure.

"Of course, Miss Bennet," he said, standing up. "You may take as much time as you wish. I am in no hurry."

"I hope you do not despise me for not being able to make up my mind."

"Not at all. I think sometimes it is better not to rush into something you might regret."

An awkward silence fell between them. Bingley rubbed his hand against the back of his neck and looked at the floor.

Elizabeth came to her feet. "I should go and fetch my sister."

Mr. Bingley nodded and gave her a genuine smile for the first time since he had come into the room.

∞ ∞ ∞

The Bingleys beat a hasty retreat, leaving Elizabeth to face Jane and tell her the unpleasant truth.

"Before you ask: yes, Mr. Bingley started to propose and yes, I didn't allow him to continue."

"But Lizzy, are you out of your mind? I thought that was your whole purpose in coming to London."

Elizabeth shook her head. "I am not certain that was ever the case." The tears that had threatened to pour out since Mr. Darcy had walked out now suddenly rose to the surface. "Oh, Jane, it is all such a terrible muddle. I am not in love with Mr. Bingley at all. I am in love with Mr. Darcy. Oh, what shall I do?"

Chapter 20

arcy was partaking of breakfast at Rosings, when a letter was brought in for him on a salver.

"That must be from Fitzwilliam," said Lady Catherine. "Read it and tell me at once what day they are planning to arrive."

The careless scrawl was not Richard's, however. Darcy knew whose it was, and he did not think he would be able to read it.

"It is not from Fitzwilliam. It is from a friend. I expect it is news of his impending nuptials." He put the letter aside. "I have no interest in reading it now."

"No, indeed. There is so much to arrange for Georgiana's wedding, you cannot be expected to show an interest in someone else's. He ought to have been more considerate."

Darcy nodded, for once agreeing with his aunt. Why had Bingley written to him here? Darcy looked towards the letter and resolved that he would not read it, not until Georgiana's wedding was over. He did not want to know about his friend's happiness and future plans, nor of his joy at being with Miss Bennet. It was even probable that Bingley would expect him to attend the wedding, which was out of the question.

Darcy was almost tempted to burn the letter. He could claim later that he had not received it until it was too late – he could blame it on his aunt, perhaps. Well, why not? It was as good an excuse as any.

Anything to avoid seeing the happiness on the face of the woman he loved as she married someone else.

∞ ∞ ∞

Elizabeth arrived in Hunsford in the afternoon and was delighted to see Charlotte's familiar face. Charlotte embraced her warmly and the two of them went into the rectory to catch up on each other's news.

"I'm sorry you will not see Mr. Collins this afternoon, Lizzy. He is at Rosings, consulting with Lady Catherine. You have come at a busy time, in fact. There is to be a wedding, you know. Miss Georgiana Darcy is to marry her cousin, Colonel Fitzwilliam."

Elizabeth's heartbeat picked up at the sound of the Darcy name.

"Indeed? Is she by any chance related to the same Mr. Darcy you wrote to me about?"

"He is her brother." Charlotte gasped. "Oh, I had not thought about it, but that might prove a little awkward. However, I do not see how you can avoid it."

"Avoid what?" A moment's thought brought her to the realization that, if she was here when the wedding took place, she would be bound to run into Mr. Darcy.

"Avoid Mr. Darcy. We are invited to dinner at Rosings tonight, and Mr. Darcy will be there. I know you wrote to tell me you had quarreled, but I hope you have made it up, because there is no escape from talking to him."

Elizabeth heart gave a sudden twist. Mr. Darcy was here now? How could it be? She had escaped both London and Longbourn to avoid any association with Mr. Darcy, only to find him here! She felt mortified. What if he were to think she had followed him here? It was not to be borne!

She stood up and began to pace, considering what she should do. Every instinct told her to pack her bags and flee, but how was she to explain it, when she had only just arrived? It would only draw attention and stir up needless suspicions.

"I don't understand, Lizzy," said Charlotte. "What have I said to upset you? Your fight with him cannot have been that bad, surely?"

"No, no. It is not that. It is nothing at all. It is just that I am not feeling well."

"Come, Lizzy, we have been friends for many years. I know you better than that." It took her a few minutes, but Charlotte was sensible and was able to puzzle it out. "I suppose you are still angry with him. I had forgotten that it was Mr. Darcy who destroyed your chance with Mr. Bingley."

"I cannot possibly see him. Not tonight. You must beg forgiveness from Lady Catherine."

"She will be displeased. Can you not bring yourself to come? You need not speak to him much, you know, beyond the barest civilities."

Elizabeth shook her head vigorously. "I cannot."

"If you are determined, then you cannot go tonight. I will say you are too tired after your journey. But you cannot continue to stay in Hunsford and avoid going to Rosings. It would be an insult to Lady Catherine. Mr. Collins will not put up with it."

"I know. I simply need time to get used to the idea that Mr. Darcy is here. The next time we are invited, I will be prepared to be civil."

At this moment, Mr. Collins came in, huffing and puffing. "We must make haste. We cannot be late for Lady Catherine. Are you planning to change, Cousin Elizabeth? You cannot appear before her in your travelling clothes. You must go upstairs quickly. Charlotte, why did you not tell her to change?"

"Lizzy is exhausted after her long journey, Mr. Collins. I do not think she will be able to attend dinner at Rosings."

Mr. Collins' eyes bulged. "But Lady Catherine is expecting her. I told her—"

"As you can see clearly, Mr. Collins, Lizzy is wretched about it. She will not say it, but I am certain it pains her greatly to be missing dinner at Lady Catherine's. However, I am sure you would not wish Lizzy to fall asleep while Lady Catherine is talking to her."

Mr. Collins looked horrified. "Fall asleep while Lady Catherine--! Certainly not! That would deeply offend her Ladyship. No, I see it now. You are quite right. Cousin, you must be strong. You must resist temptation. You cannot visit Lady Catherine if you are in danger of falling asleep. You cannot trespass on her ladyship's hospitality if you are too tired. You must remain in the rectory. Have no fear. I will make certain Lady Catherine will invite you again before you leave."

Elizabeth pressed her lips together to stop herself from laughing. "Why, that is very kind of you, Cousin."

Mr. Collins bowed deeply.

"Come, then, Mr. Collins. Let us prepare ourselves. You do not wish to be late." Charlotte turned to Elizabeth. "I will apologize to Lady Catherine on your behalf, Lizzy."

"It is really most unfortunate that you are missing this delightful opportunity to dine with Lady Catherine. Would you care for a book to provide solace? May I suggest *Fordyce's Sermons*? It is a most enlightening book."

"You are very kind, Mr. Collins," said Elizabeth, inclining her head, "but I have brought my own book with me from London."

"Come, Mr. Collins," urged his wife.

"Yes, yes, my dear Charlotte. You are quite right. We cannot arrive late."

Elizabeth breathed a sigh of relief as the carriage Lady Catherine had sent to bring them to Rosings labored slowly down the cobbled lane.

With a sigh of relief, she watched until the carriage had driven away. She was glad to have some time to herself to reflect on this unexpected turn of events.

It was a lovely spring evening. After the noise and crowds of London, the tranquil verdure was beautiful in the late afternoon sun. It beckoned to her, and, unable to resist, she quickly went up to her room to put on her bonnet and spencer and do what she always did when she felt unhappy. She would go for a walk.

∞ ∞ ∞

The letter sat on the mantlepiece, staring down at him. Darcy threw himself on his bed and did his best to ignore it. He would open it at some point, he supposed, but it would not be today.

He felt it like a presence in the room. The more he tried to forget about it, the more he was tempted to get up and read it. He did his best to distract himself, but even trying to read a book of poems did not stop him from wondering about the contents of that letter. Finally, unable to put it out of his mind, he broke the seal and unfolded it.

Dear Darcy,

I have news for you. I proposed to Miss Bennet and she turned me down. I thought I would be devastated, but the fact is, Darcy, you were right as usual. My obsession with Miss Bennet was nothing but a foolish notion that has evaporated completely. I would never have imagined it, but the moment she rejected me, I knew it was the right

thing. The worst of it is, I did not care at all. You will say I told you so,
that I am the worst kind of scoundrel, and I will deserve it. I will never
ask for a lady's hand unless I have consulted you first. You know me
better than I know myself.

There is more bad news to be conveyed. I have landed myself in a spot
of trouble. In fact, I have done the worst thing possible. I have fallen in
love with Miss Bennet's sister, Mrs. Munstead. A married lady! If you
needed proof of how foolish I am, you now have it. If you could see her,
you would understand. She is the most beautiful woman I have ever
seen. Darcy, she is an angel. I know it is entirely hopeless, of course, but
I think of her day and night. The feelings I had for Miss Bennet pale in
comparison. Oh, Darcy, what am I to do?

Your foolish friend, Bingley

Darcy threw down the letter in disgust. For once he had no
patience with Bingley's disgraceful scrapes. It beggared belief that he
had abandoned Miss Bennet for her married sister. Though to be fair
to Bingley, it did not seem that it was his fault alone. What was it that
Bingley had said?

She turned me down.

Why on earth would Miss Bennet do such a thing when she had
been wishing for such an outcome for so long?

Hope reared its head inside him. Was it possible she no longer
cared about Bingley? Then perhaps Darcy had a chance after all.

He dismissed the idea immediately. The fact that she no longer
wanted to marry Bingley did not mean that she would be more
inclined to marry Darcy. There was no logic in thinking that way. He
did not understand her reasons for rejecting Bingley, but there was

nothing in that letter that could possibly lead to any optimism on his part. Except, of course, the fact that she would not be marrying Bingley.

He had no idea how to react. How could he know what her rejection of Bingley meant? It would not become clear unless he spoke to Miss Bennet. He could only speculate, which meant nothing at all.

Darcy wished now that he had not read the letter. It had destroyed his tranquility completely, throwing him into a fever of impatience. He wanted to leave Rosings and go to Longbourn immediately, but Georgiana and Richard were arriving soon, and they were getting married, and he was supposed to give Georgiana away. He did not even know if Miss Bennet was still in London or whether she had returned to Meryton.

Miss Bennet would have to wait.

He tried to curb his restlessness by going on a quick walk before dinner. Walking in the countryside made him think of Miss Bennet. Everything made him think of Miss Bennet. If he could have plucked her from his thoughts he would have, but she had taken hold of him mind and heart and he was too helplessly besotted to extricate himself.

He walked for some time, then, as he remembered that his aunt was expecting him for dinner, he decided to make his way back. It would not do to be late, particularly since his aunt had guests. Not that he felt much inclined to dine with the disagreeable Mr. Collins. He would be yet another reminder of Miss Bennet. He recalled every word she had said about her cousin's studied compliments.

The memory brought a smile to his face. In spite of his pain and uncertainty, she could make him laugh, even now. She had always brought joy to his heart.

As he made his way to the copse of trees at the front of the house, he thought he saw something – someone. His heart gave a jolt. It could not be, of course. Yet, as the sun set, the outline of her figure was as real as anything he had ever seen. No other woman looked quite like this. He was sure it was a delusion, born of hope, that if he blinked, she would disappear. He moved quickly in her direction, keeping his gaze on her, afraid to look away. As he drew closer, he could hear the scrape of her half-boots on the ground, along with the quiet swish of her skirt.

It was someone else, of course, someone who resembled her. *She* could not be here.

The woman must have heard his footsteps. She stopped and turned, and then her beautiful eyes were upon him. A sharp sensation whizzed through him and he was fixed to the spot, unable to move, unable to breathe.

"Mr. Darcy!"

It was her, in the flesh. There was no mistaking that slightly husky voice.

"Miss Bennet."

"I thought you would be at dinner. I—did not expect to encounter you out here. I—" She chewed at her lip and looked pained.

He sought for something to say, anything.

"When did you arrive?"

"This afternoon."

She knew he would be at dinner, but she had decided not to attend. It hurt him to know that.

"You were avoiding me." The words spilled out of his mouth. He had not meant to say them.

She shook her head. "No— I was tired from the journey – not fit for company – I could not – dinner at Rosings was beyond me."

He nodded. "Yes, yes, of course." Still, if the situation had been reversed, he would have rushed over at once, no matter how tired he was.

They fell into silence.

"Well – I should go—" she gestured towards the parsonage.

He refused to let her go.

"Is your sister in good health?"

"Yes," she replied.

"And Mr. Munstead?"

"Yes. In very good health."

"Do you know your way back to the parsonage? I could accompany you."

He cringed. It was a stupid question. If she said yes—.

"Yes."

"Oh." He had braced for her answer, but it was still a blow that she did not want him.

"I mean, I know my way, but you are welcome to accompany me."

∞ ∞ ∞

Elizabeth took her leave of Mr. Darcy at the end of the lane and hurried inside. The walk back had been so awkward, she was sure he thought her a complete imbecile. She had been so flustered at encountering him that she had been reduced to monosyllabic utterances. She could not manage anything more. The emotions that buffeted her were too strong to allow for sensible conversation.

Fortunately, that first encounter was over. She could now meet with him again with equanimity. Next time she saw him, she would be calm and polite, and would give no indication of the tumult that was raging inside her.

Once again, she was glad to have the luxury of time to herself to recover from her ordeal. Having regained her composure once again, Elizabeth settled in for the evening, trying her best not to dwell on her encounter with Mr. Darcy. She had just poured herself some tea and a slice of cherry pie for her dinner, when she was roused by the sound of the doorbell. Thinking it might be a parishioner wanting to speak to Mr. Collins, she paid it no attention, beyond hoping it was not something urgent that would require interrupting Mr. Collins' dinner at Rosings.

Moments later, she was just partaking of a mouthful of pie when, the maid appeared in the doorway.

"Mr. Darcy to see you, Miss Bennet."

The familiar form of Mr. Darcy appeared in the doorway. Elizabeth was all amazement. She jumped to her feet so quickly she dropped her pie on the floor, and, swallowing too fast, choked on a crumb. A fit of intense coughing resulted as she tried to dislodge the morsel from her throat.

"Miss Bennet!"

In two strides he was at her side, holding her by one shoulder and striking her back with his palm.

Her eyes watering, she waved him away.

Darcy quickly went to the table and poured her a cup of tea, doused it with milk, and handed it to her with an unsteady hand.

She could not imagine a more inopportune moment. His hand closed over hers to steady it as she sipped the tea and tried to put a stop to the coughing. She sputtered, spilling the tea. He took the cup from her and put it on the table, then helped her sit down and perched on the arm of the chair, rubbing her back.

Finally, the fit subsided, but her breathing still came in great gasps. It was impossible to breathe normally, constrained as she was by his closeness. She closed her eyes and clasped her hands together in an effort to bring her errant pulse into control.

"Thank you, Mr. Darcy. I am quite recovered now."

She wanted him to move away, but he seemed disinclined to do so. Truth be told, she did not want him to move, either, but she was only too aware of the impropriety of their situation, even if he did not seem to notice it.

"Would you like some tea, Mr. Darcy? I will have a cup brought for you."

Only now did he seem to become aware of his position. He stood up hastily and seated himself in Mr. Collins' armchair. He looked very different from Mr. Collins, she noted idly, as her thoughts began to resume some semblance of normalcy. She had to fight an absurd desire to giggle.

"Thank you, Miss Bennet, but I intend to dine at Rosings."

She did not know what to say to that, except that he was very late for dinner.

A silence fell on the room and the ticking of the clock sounded thunderous in her ears. She sought something to say, since he did not show any sign of leaving.

"How have you been feeling about your hard-won freedom?" she said.

"Well enough. I am still not quite used to it." His mind was not on his answer, however. He seemed completely preoccupied.

He stood up again and walked over to the window, where he stared out into the deepening darkness. He was standing with his back to her. Elizabeth took advantage of this to smooth down her hair and straighten her clothes, which had been disturbed by her coughing.

"It has come to my attention, Miss Bennet, that my friend Mr. Bingley has proposed to you."

Elizabeth started. Whatever she had expected, it was not this. Had he come to scold her?

"If you have come to lecture me, I would ask you to refrain from doing so. If you know that your friend proposed, you should also know also that I refused him."

"Are you completely certain?"

"Of course I am certain that I refused him."

"Do you think that is a wise course of action?"

She could not trust herself to say another word. She looked down and pretended to be examining the tea in her teacup. Foolish, foolish tears. They had sprung up in her eyes and were blinding her. What else had she expected when Mr. Darcy had come in? Naturally he was here to ensure that she should accept Mr. Bingley's offer.

Mr. Darcy left his position at the window. After pacing the room in agitation, he sat down again. Elizabeth felt the awkwardness of the moment intensely. A strong stubbornness in her, however, prevented her from trying to defend herself. It was not her fault that Mr. Bingley had taken an interest in her. She had done nothing in particular to fix his interest, despite Mrs. Bennet's urgings, unless one counted the time she had walked to Netherfield and been taken sick. She braced herself for Mr. Darcy's censure.

Mr. Darcy jumped up and came towards her. He sat at the edge of a chair, just inches away from her.

"Miss Bennet – Elizabeth – I can repress my feelings no longer. You must allow me to tell you how ardently I admire and love you. Almost from the first moments of our acquaintance I have come to feel for you a passionate admiration and regard."

She stared, not quite absorbing his words.

"You were right to chide me, Miss Bennet, for coming between you and Mr. Bingley. I had thought my reasons noble, but I know now that I was prompted as much by jealousy as by concern for my friend.

Though I did not know it then myself, I wanted to separate you. I could not bear to stand by and see Bingley make you his wife."

"I am not sure I understand your meaning, Mr. Darcy."

"What I am trying to say – not very eloquently, I'm afraid – is that you have bewitched me, body and soul, Miss Bennet – Elizabeth -- and I can no longer hold back. I know my reputation is not the best at this point. I have just left jail and my name is on everyone's lips. However, if you could bring yourself to overlook that, if you could possibly consider—" His voice broke. All the agony, all the exhaustion of the past three years seemed to find their cumulation in this moment. "I am a broken man, Miss Bennet, but if you could bring yourself to consider me, I would be eternally grateful. I beg you most fervently to relieve my suffering and consent to be my wife. If you do not wish me to continue in this manner, one word from you will silence me on this subject forever."

Elizabeth trembled at his words, but seeing the anxiety in his eyes, forced herself to speak. Her voice as she answered was none too steady.

"You must not think for a moment that I agree with your summary of your situation, Mr. Darcy. You have been through a great deal of pain, none of it caused by yourself." She took a deep breath, knowing he was waiting for her answer, and reached out to put her hand to his cheek.

"There is nothing in the world that will give me more pleasure than to marry you, Mr. Darcy."

The look of incredulity on his face was enough to tell her all she needed to know. He grasped her hand in both of his and covered it with kisses, then he leaned over to fasten his lips on hers.

∞ ∞ ∞

Several minutes later they were startled by the sound of a teacup falling to the floor.

Elizabeth stared at the cup and began to laugh, and soon Darcy joined her, the rich sound of his laughter filling the room.

"I do believe you have spilled the tea again, Miss Bennet – Elizabeth." He looked at her with tenderness. "My dearest Elizabeth."

"I am afraid I will have to ring for someone to clean it up," she said, regretfully. "Mr. Collins will not be pleased."

At the thought of Mr. Collins, Elizabeth gave a start. "Mr. Darcy, you do realize they are expecting you at Rosings, don't you?"

He smiled. "Yes, I do believe you are right. Put on a bonnet, Miss Bennet. I want you to come with me."

"Oh, no. I cannot. I am not dressed."

"I will decide whether you are properly dressed or not. If it were up to me at this moment, you would not be dressed at all, but unfortunately we cannot always have everything we wish for."

Elizabeth blushed at the thought. She still could not believe that she had just consented to marry Mr. Darcy.

He gave her a little tug. "Come, my dearest Elizabeth. I don't want any further delay. I want to announce our engagement to the world. I won't give you a chance to change your mind."

"I have no intention of changing my mind, Mr. Darcy. I am afraid you will have to get used to having me at your side for a very long time."

He pulled her towards him and kissed her again. "Then you will make me the happiest man in the world."

Epilogue

*I*t was a warm day in May, the sky deep azure and the sun beaming down on the carriage. Bluebells lined the road and were scattered under the shades of the majestic oaks standing to both sides. As she passed one of the great trees, a thrush burst into song. Elizabeth's heart swelled. It was the most beautiful sound in the world.

She and Mr. Bennet were the sole occupants of Mr. Darcy's carriage. Mrs. Bennet, her sisters and Charlotte were already at the chapel, and Mr. Collins, of course, was there to get in the way of the Bishop who would be officiating over the wedding.

"Are you absolutely certain this is what you want, Lizzy?" asked Mr. Bennet, not for the first time.

"Yes, papa."

"Are you sure you are not doing this out of some sense of obligation? Trying to be sensible and doing your duty? Hm?"

Elizabeth laughed. "Of course not. There is nothing sensible about wanting to marry Mr. Darcy. He has the most dreadful relations, especially his aunt. I am marrying him because I love him."

"At least you aren't too blind not to notice his relatives. If you are sure you are in love, then there is nothing further to be said on the subject."

Elizabeth could sense the sadness coming from her father. She knew it would be difficult for him that she would be living so far away.

"You must promise to exert yourself and come to Pemberley frequently."

"If there is a good library there, as you claim there is, you can be certain I will avail myself of its contents. I will visit whenever I feel truly starved of intelligent conversation, which will probably mean quite often."

The way from the rectory seemed endless to Elizabeth as they drove up the long driveway to Rosings. Mr. Darcy was waiting for her, and so was the beginning of a completely new way of life.

∞ ∞ ∞

Fitzwilliam Darcy stood in the private chapel at Rosings Park. While his ancestors might have used it frequently, Lady Catherine did not care to worship in private. She preferred to attend the village church, where she could oversee Mr. Collins and make sure he had not deviated from the sermon she had outlined for him, and where she could also affirm her presence to her parishioners.

Darcy had not been in the chapel for many years, since he was a child. When he had last played here, it had been dusty with disuse, the wooden benches perfect for hide and seek. Today it had been readied for the occasion. The old benches had been polished, the worn cushions of the Prie Deu chair replaced with new tapestry, the stained-glass windows washed until they were gleaming, and the marble floor was scrubbed until Darcy could almost see his reflection.

Only a few people occupied the seats. The Bennets, of course, were here, with Jane and Mr. Munstead. Lady Matlock sat with Lady Catherine to her right and Anne to her left. Mr. Collins occupied one of the side benches with Mrs. Collins. He was looking even more ingratiatingly servile than usual, hoping, not doubt, that the bishop who was performing the ceremony would recommend him for some special post and transform Mr. Collins from a toad into a prince, however unlikely such a prospect might be.

Darcy waited, with Richard Fitzwilliam by his side. The door to the chapel opened and Darcy's breath caught, but it was only the curate binging in some flowers.

"I don't know what is taking them so long." Lady Catherine's voice was tight with disapproval. "Anne is going to catch her death if she has to wait in this cold chapel much longer."

Then finally the door opened, and there were the two brides, accompanied by the men who were to give them away. The Earl of Matlock was resplendent in his regalia, with Mr. Bennet looking much plainer but surprisingly elegant in a well-tailored court dress.

Darcy's gaze turned to rest on the enchanting figure of Miss Elizabeth Bennet, soon to become Mrs. Darcy. A wave of intense pleasure went through him at the thought. She strode into the church as if planning to take one of her long walks through the mud. Darcy's lips twitched in amusement. Nothing would dampen her spirit, not even an Earl looking forbidding as he marched down the aisle with poor Georgiana struggling to catch up with him.

The Earl had objected much more strenuously than Lady Catherine to Darcy's choice of a bride and had argued with him fiercely for several days, threatening to boycott the marriage. He had continued to insist that Darcy could do better -- until Darcy had threatened never to marry and to leave Pemberley to a distant cousin. It was a gamble, because the Earl had no vested interest in Pemberley, particularly now that his son was marrying into a large fortune.

Luckily it worked. Seeing there was no swaying Darcy on the issue, Lord Matlock offered his congratulations.

"The main thing is that you have returned to us, that you are free from any stains on your character, and that you can come back to reclaim Pemberley."

Not for the first time, Darcy was grateful for his uncle's kindness. He had provided him with refuge in Cornwall when he had needed it, and now, when he could have made matters difficult for him, he had chosen to overlook Elizabeth Bennet's less desirable connections.

Not so Lady Catherine. From his aunt, he faced much greater opposition. Her first reaction was to refuse to allow him to marry in Rosings.

"Very well, then. I am sure we can hold the ceremony at Netherfield. As a matter of fact, I would prefer it. Be warned, however, that if it takes place in Netherfield, it will still be a double wedding, and you will not be invited. I am certain my uncle will not be happy that you refused to attend his son's wedding."

In the end, Lady Catherine gave in. She wanted to play an important role in arranging Richard's wedding, knowing it would further enhance her status to have an Earl in attendance. However, her attitude towards Elizabeth was cold, and she was frequently overheard to mutter comments about that "impertinent girl" who would be "polluting the shades" of Pemberley. Fortunately, Elizabeth was too happy to care, and she seemed to derive a great deal of amusement from Lady Catherine's remarks.

Dearest, loveliest, Elizabeth! Anyone else would have been cowed by his aunt, but Elizabeth took it all in her stride. When he had apologized for his aunt's poor conduct, she had laughed.

"You are not the only one with uncivil relatives." Her mouth quirked playfully, and he was sorely tempted to put aside convention and shower kisses on those impudent lips.

"We are both cursed with them – as I am only too aware -- but we will not let them affect our happiness. We are both perfectly capable of dealing with them."

Meanwhile, Mrs. Bennet, sitting as far away from Lady Catherine as was possible in the small chapel, was whispering loudly as she watched her daughter approach.

"Have you ever seen any bride more beautiful than my Lizzy? I always knew she was pretty for a good reason. That was exactly what I said to Mr. Bennet. I told him she was destined for great things. To think that Mr. Darcy, whom we thought a nobody, is the nephew of an Earl!"

Darcy tried to ignore the whispering, but the chapel echoed, and he was certain no one could have missed her remarks. Still, he had to agree that Elizabeth was the most beautiful bride he had ever seen. All his senses fixed on her as she approached. Her dark eyes were laughing, even now on this solemn occasion. No doubt she was amused by her mother's words. Suddenly he, too, wanted to laugh, from pure joy.

Then she was standing next to him, and as her hand reached out to clasp his, he knew everything was as it should be. For three years he had wandered and had cursed the fate that had forced him to do so. Little had he known that fate had other plans for him. His world was right now. He would never forgive himself for what had happened to Wickham, even if the courts had not found him guilty, but with Elizabeth at his side, he could begin to heal, and to build a new future.

He stood straight as the Bishop began to speak.

"Do you, Fitzwilliam Edward John Darcy take this woman..."

"I do."

And he did.

∞ ∞ ∞

As the carriage drew away, Mr. and Mrs. Darcy shook the rice that had been thrown at them from their clothes and settled in for the long journey southwest. Darcy took her hand and linked their fingers, then gently brought down his lips to taste hers. Her lips were sweet and tender, and he soon found himself drowning in them. Only his awareness that there was an outrider behind them and a coachman in front stopped him from taking full advantage of the moment.

He would have to be patient. There would be many nights and days when they could be together without restrictions.

He drew his lips reluctantly away and wrapped an arm around her shoulders, drawing her close, fixing the blanket around them.

"Well, Mrs. Darcy, I do seem to recall that you showed a great deal of interest in walking on the moors in Cornwall. While I may not particularly care about walking on the moors alone, I will admit that there is a certain appeal in exploring them in the company of a beautiful young lady. What do you say to that?"

Elizabeth's eyes danced in that special way that he loved so much.

"I will say, sir, that I have always wanted to discover more about Cornwall. However, to be completely honest, at this particular point in time, I am much more interested in discovering more about my husband, the mysterious Mr. Darcy."

THE END

About Monica

Monica can be described as a gypsy-wanderer, opening her eyes to life in London and travelling ever since. She spent many years in the USA before coming back full circle to London, thus proving that the world is undeniably round.

Monica's first novel was *An Improper Suitor*, a humorous Regency. Since then, she has written two traditional Jane Austen sequels: *The Other Mr. Darcy* and *The Darcy Cousins* (both published by Sourcebooks) and contributed a sequel to *Emma* in Laurel Ann Nattress's anthology *Jane Austen Made Me Do It* (Ballantine). She has also published a futuristic *Pride and Prejudice* spoof, *Steampunk Darcy*.

Then came her popular series, *The Darcy Novels*, which are traditional Pride and Prejudice 'what-if' variations focusing on Darcy's transformation through his love for Elizabeth. The novels can be read independently but might be more scrumptious when read together.

Monica Fairview is an ex-professor who enjoys researching the Regency era. She has also discovered that the Victorian period can be jolly good fun if viewed with retro-vision and rose-colored goggles, and she also loves the Edwardian period as exemplified by Downton Abbey. She loves visiting historical mansions, watching period drama and trying to understand her two cats, but finds her husband, her impossible volleyball-wielding daughter, and her high-achieving stepdaughter tolerable as well.

If you'd like to find out more about Monica, you can find her at
Author.to/FairviewDarcyNovel
Blog: http://austenvariations.com
www.monicafairview.blogspot.co.uk
Facebook: http://www.facebook.com/monica.fairview
Twitter @Monica_Fairview

Printed in Great Britain
by Amazon